"The Sorcerer

W.S.Gilbert

Throughout this book we have tried to present the recipes in a style and form which, as far as possible, reflect the diverse way in which they were presented by the artists. The older recipes in particular are not tried and tested, and readers are advised to use their instinct and informed judgement to adapt and modify them for the modern day kitchen!

David and Melvyn

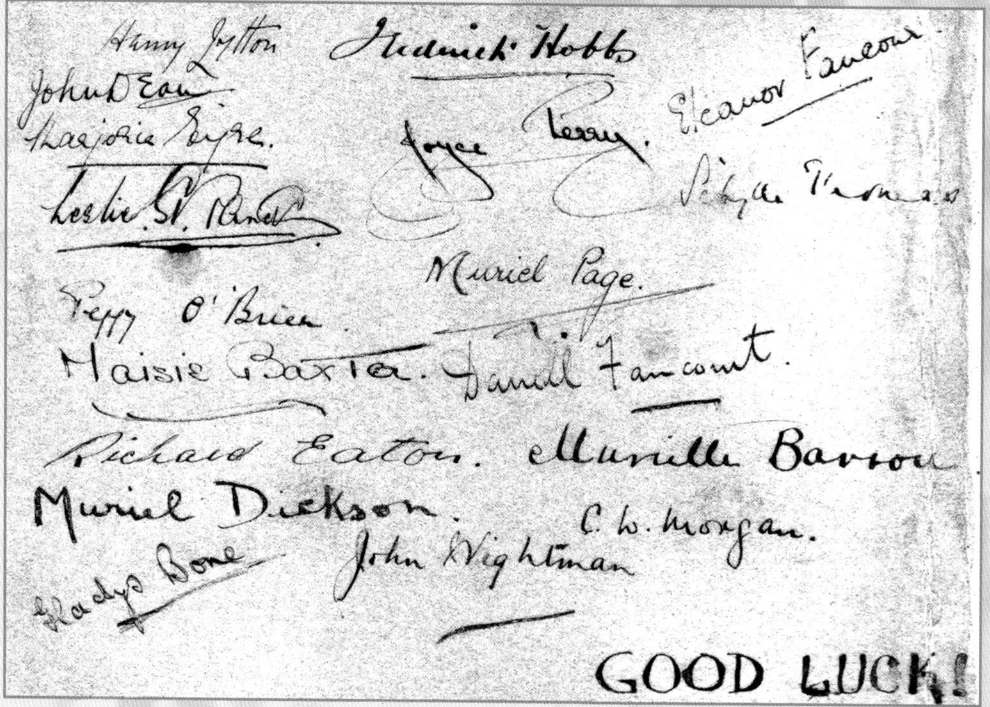

ISBN 978-1-910864-04-3

First published in the United Kingdom in 2016 by
The Choir Press

Contents

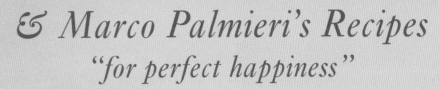

& Marco Palmieri's Recipes
"for perfect happiness"

Thomas Round

Lady Blanche: "Princess Ida"

From the recipe book of

Bertha Lewis.

Tipsy Cake.

1 moulded sponge cake a few days
old sherry or raisin wine to soak
4 tablespoonful of Brandy.
2 oz sweet almonds blanched
1 pkt Bird's custard powder
2 oz white sugar
¼pt cream
¼ pt milk
Stand cake firm in glass dish cut
bottom level. Make small hole in
top & pour into it & over it enough
wine mixed with brandy to soak
it nicely. Let it soak for 2 hrs &
then stick all over with almonds cut
in strips. Make custard & pour
when cool into the dish round the cake
not over it.

Horseradish Cream

1 horseradish (grated)
6 d cream
2 teaspoonfuls caster sugar
2 tablespoonfuls vinegar. pepper
& salt to taste.

Hot Cakes.

1pt milk 2 eggs teaspoonful salt-
one of bak: pow: with enough flour to
make like sponge cake. Beat milk &
eggs salt & powder well together, then
add flour slowly beating all the
time. Bake in small cake tins in
a quick oven. When done split-open
& butter.

Shrewsbury Biscuits.

¼ lb butter.
¼ lb caster sugar
½ " flour.
1 egg - pinch salt. 1 teaspoonful grated
lemon rind.
Method. Beat butter & sugar to cream
then add them the egg & rind. Beat
together & stir smoothly. Flour a board
& turn paste on it. Roll out as thin
as possible Cut in rounds. Put on
greased tin & bake 10 min:

Foreword: Mike Leigh O.B.E.

Photo by Myrna Suárez

There's a much-loved theatrical story. Two frequently out-of-work actors meet ...

"I say, old bean – I hear you've got a job."

"Yes, indeed I have."

"Well done! What are the wages like?"

"Dreadful, old chap, but never mind – there's a practical pork pie in the Second Act."

Real food eaten as part of the dramatic action has often saved the bacon of many an impoverished, undernourished thesp, especially on tour.

Eating out can be prohibitive for all but the wealthiest of performers, and, as this appetising book testifies, members of the D'Oyly Carte Company, although presumably paid reasonable wages, were endlessly inventive and resourceful at survival by self-catering.

This is just as well, as a brief gastronomic tour of the Savoy Operas reveals that Gilbert provides little by way of the "practical pork pie".

There are, of course, the famous rasher of bacon and the pork chop in *Cox & Box*, which the Company included in its repertoire for many years. But both these promising comestibles are summarily thrown out of the window by the eponymous heroes.

Trial by Jury yields nothing, although the Defendant does reveal himself to be a confirmed gourmand in his smug justification of his philandering. And in *The Sorcerer*, all anybody gets to ingest is the "spiked" tea, as the villagers never get round to enjoying the scrumptious eggs-and-ham spread they so enthusiastically sing about.

Absolutely nothing is eaten in *H.M.S. Pinafore*, either, despite Little Buttercup's mouth-watering list of her wares (which, curiously, none of the ship's crew seem disposed to purchase); and Frederic's coming-of-age party, which opens *The Pirates of Penzance* would appear to be "booze only, no nibbles", after which no more refreshment is taken for the rest of the opera. (In my 2015 ENO production, we did have the pirates relieve the Major-General's servants of the Stanley family picnic, with the Act One curtain coming down on the brigands eagerly unpacking the hampers.)

The strict diet continues through *Patience* and *Iolanthe*, with culinary information restricted to the news that Bunthorne has been spotted in the dairy, eating fresh butter with a tablespoon, and that the Lord Chancellor's nocturnal cravings involve foodstuffs many and various, not least at the hands of the pastry cook.

Only when we get to *Princess Ida* is luncheon laid on. This includes cold roast lamb, but there's hardly enough time for anybody on stage to sample it.

As for *The Mikado*, not a morsel passes anybody's lips. However, when the Mikado returns for the execution, after what he describes as "a capital lunch", it's interesting to speculate that, as he and Katisha have been offstage for a relatively short time, they may perhaps have dined only on the sushi and sashimi, rather than taking the full bento box.

Ruddigore is another foodless feast, limited to the peppermint rock Rose Maybud has procured for old Gaffer Gadderby, and her gift of that damaged apple, which young Richard Dauntless so ungraciously returns to her, uneaten.

On goes the famine. *The Yeomen of the Guard* yields nothing more incidental than the cook's brain-pan in Jack Point's unexplained joke, and the sausage given by the Rich Councillor to the Poor Wit, while *The Gondoliers* pays lip service variously to buns, rusks, macaroni, peaches, sugar-plums and ices, compares plum pudding to Life itself, and makes no less than ten references to alcoholic beverages of various kinds. (In a remarkably radical innovation, however, Anthony Besch, in his 1968 D'Oyly Carte production, had the Plaza-Toros actually eat pasta in Act One.)

With *Utopia Ltd*, we find ourselves back with the narcotic problems of the philtre-laced tea in *The Sorcerer*. Does Gilbert's stage direction at the top of Act One – the maidens are discovered "enjoying themselves in lotus-eating fashion" – mean that they are actually eating lotuses? If so, their ability to deal as coherently as they do with the rest of the action of the opera is, strictly speaking, impossible. Anyhow, no real food is eaten, not even at Utopia's first South Pacific "Drawing Room".

Which brings us, finally and ironically, to the last of the operas, the one least performed by the Company, and the only one with dramatically essential edibles. This is, of course, *The Grand Duke*.

The hors d'oeuvre to this, Gilbert's final departure from his nil by mouth regime, is the wedding breakfast Ernest Dummkopf's troupe is discovered "enjoying" (Gilbert's stage direction) as the opera opens, and which they continue to munch for some time into the action.

That is, until we come to the Holy Grail – the only true "practical pork pie" element in all the operas, those dastardly sausage rolls the conspirators are obliged to eat by way of their secret sign.

In fact, only Ludwig actually eats one on stage, although in a delightful amateur production I saw recently, large supplies of the delicacy were produced during the *Sausage Roll* song, enabling the entire company to partake, to great comic effect. (In the Finborough Theatre version, trayloads were also offered round, but only Ludwig ate one.)

And so, courtesy of the inspired Messrs Steadman and Tarran, let us savour the joys and delight of the valiant pan-wielding Savoyards of these glorious pages.

Those of us lucky enough to have been their devoted fans over the years can now enhance our memories of their spirited performances with greater understanding. For, as we know, an army marches on its stomach.

Introduction by Melvyn Tarran

Joy Garland and the story of *Cookery à la Carte*

Joy

News had reached Joy about my Gilbert and Sullivan Restaurant *Sullivan's*, which I had opened in 1979 in the Sussex village of Hassocks; she lived close by in Hurstpierpoint and came to visit us one morning in her wonderfully theatrical way and with a speaking voice to match! She had an enormous presence and was keen to know "Were you in the D'Oyly Carte?"

In 1932, Joy had successfully auditioned for Rupert D'Oyly Carte and joined the Chorus which, he maintained, was the back-bone of the Company and from where new principal artists were often promoted.

One can imagine how this bubbly young lady soon made friends within the D'Oyly Carte Company and it was not long before Sir Henry Lytton became one of her admirers. Then of course, there were the "stage door Johnnies" – wealthy young professionals in their smart black tuxedoes and bow-ties, seeking to acquaint themselves with Carte's young ladies. Browsing through the many snapshots in Joy's photo albums, it's clear that these were very special times.

In 1934, everything changed when Joy was swept off her feet by a young neurologist named Hugh Garland who she agreed to marry. Rupert D'Oyly Carte was disappointed to see her go as he had hoped she would take over some of the smaller principal roles; on leaving the Company, Joy was

presented with a green leather-bound book, inscribed in gold and entitled *Cookery à la Carte* in which her colleagues had hand-written some of their favourite recipes.

Throughout their lives, Hugh and Joy kept in contact with the D'Oyly Carte Opera Company and would often entertain at their home in Leeds. Hugh would greet everyone with one of his potent Gin & Grapefruit cocktails while Joy's various hot curries were simmering in the oven. After dinner, drinks would continue to flow and the evening would end with songs round the grand piano.

Years later, Joy gave me her treasured *Cookery à la Carte* and from then on, I had the idea of putting together a G&S Cook Book. I embarked on it's compilation some years ago, but I had a busy life and as the project grew I thought I might need some assistance; my good friend David Steadman liked what I was planning and offered his help. I was mad keen to have David on board and in no time at all, he was getting yet more recipes from numerous D'Oyly Carte artists he had worked with, writing up anecdotes and negotiating with a publisher.

At last, what started out with a little green book has grown into this rather larger version of *Cookery à la Carte* – I wonder what Joy would think?

Melvyn

Picnic with Fred Hobbs and Sir Henry

Lunch party with
Sir Henry Lytton

Happy Days at Oak Hall: Mary Godfrey,
Pat Leonard, David Steadman and Joy Garland

Melvyn with some of his many D'Oyly Carte guests at Oak Hall; here he hosted reunions, concerts, afternoon teas and dinners as well as welcoming visitors to the Melvyn Tarran Collection.

Valerie Masterson and Thomas Round

A D'Oyly Carte Reunion

David Steadman, Pat Leonard and John Ayldon

Donald Adams

At bunch of tenors! They include Sullivan officianado Stephen Brown (left) and Alfie Boe (right). Alfie made his professional debut with the D'Oyly Carte in 1994.

On display at Oak Hall: some of the famous Mikado kimonos by Charles Ricketts.

Many items from the Melvyn Tarran Collection were featured in the National Trust's Exhibition at Nymans in Sussex, former home of the Messel family. The Messels became related to W.S. Gilbert and his wife when Harold Messel married Lucy Gilbert's niece Leonora Gibson.

You are invited to the private view of

Gilbert and Sullivan at Nymans

An exhibition featuring the private collection of Melvyn Tarran

Wednesday 9 December 4-6pm

The Gallery at Nymans
Nymans
Handcross
West Sussex
RH17 6EB

RSVP to nymans@nationaltrust.org.uk

The exhibition will continue until 3 January 2016

The Messel's on a visit to Grim's Dyke:
Back row: Harold Messel with son, Rudolph; Leonora;
Front row: Lucy and W.S. Gilbert; Jane Gibson (Leonora's mother) with Phoebe Messel on her lap.

Copyright © National Trust

W.S. Gilbert's Sweet Tooth

W.S. Gilbert, co-founder of our feast, writer of over 70 stage works, poet, illustrator, inspirational director and wit, had a long association with D'Oyly Carte which went beyond his work as librettist. He was director of all the original Carte productions (and many revivals) of the operas he wrote with Sir Arthur Sullivan, supervised the design of costumes and sets and was the actual designer for many of the costumes in *Patience*, *Iolanthe*, *Princess Ida* and *Ruddigore*. Gilbert also appeared as a chorister (and Associate) in *Trial by Jury* in London (see picture below) and *H.M.S. Pinafore* in New York. In 1907, he became the first British playwright to be knighted for his literary works alone.

Gilbert's sweet tooth was catered for prolifically in his wife's cook-books which are full of recipes for pancakes, tarts, mousses and puddings, including Almond Cake, Mocha Tart, Iced Mango Soufflé, Apple Gatta, Champagne Truffles and Red Porridge! Such cuisine was a long way from that of his bachelor days when steak, boiled beef and bottled ale formed his staple diet.

In 1906, a Savoyard Celebration Dinner was held in Gilbert's honour. In his speech, he spoke of his "*old friend and co-worker*", Arthur Sullivan

"*... whose untimely death, in the fullness of his powers, extinguished the class of opera with which his name was so honourably identified – a composer of the rarest genius, and who, because he was a composer of the rarest genius, was as modest and unassuming as a neophyte should be, but seldom is.*"

A memory of life at Grimsdyke ...

"My parents met at Grim's Dyke House, W.S. Gilbert's last home at Old Redding, Harrow Weald, Middlesex (my father in the stables and mother the undercook. My mother was chosen to accompany W.S. Gilbert and his company to London to make sure that he was well-fed – especially to make him his favourite sweet, Treacle Tart, at which, he said, she excelled!

During the visits, she and the other servants were able to enjoy a 'box' at the first showing of whatever the occasion might have been arranged for. Yes, Gilbert did enjoy the exotic food and huge banquets were given. If these occasions happened in the heat of the summer, the whole kitchen was lined with blocks of ice ... no fridges, and not comfortable for the kitchen staff!"

Maud Hill, 1986.

"THE MIKADO". SAVOY THEATRE

THE O.P. CLUB
SAVOYARD CELEBRATION DINNER
Guest of the Evening, Mr. W. S. Gilbert
The President, Mr. Sidney Dark, *in the Chair*

Sunday, December 30, 1906, Hotel Cecil, Strand, W.C.

TOAST LIST AND PROGRAMME

Toast	**The King**
The President	
Toast	**The Savoy Opera**
The President	Mr. W. S. Gilbert
Song . . . . "I can't think why"	. . *Princess Ida*
Mr. C. Herbert Workman	
Song . . "Kind Sir, you cannot have the heart"	*The Gondoliers*
Miss Lilian Coomber	
Song . . . "Ida was a twelvemonth old"	. *Princess Ida*
Mr. Robert Evett	
Toast	**The Savoyards**
Mr. T. McDonald Rendle	Miss Rosina Brandram
	Mr. George Grossmith
Quartette . "Brightly dawns our Wedding Day"	. *The Mikado*
Miss Agnes Fraser, Miss Jessie Rose,	
Mr. Scott Russell, and Mr. Richard Temple	
Song . . . "A pair of sparkling eyes"	. *The Gondoliers*
Mr. Courtice Pounds	
Song . . . "The Moon and I"	. . *The Mikado*
Miss Isabel Jay	
Toast	**The Savoy Lovers**
Mr. Rutland Barrington	Mr. Carl Hentschel
Song . . . "The Vicar's Song"	. *The Sorcerer*
Mr. Rutland Barrington	
Song . . "The Lord Chancellor's Dream"	. *Iolanthe*
Mr. Walter Passmore	

Accompanist - Mr. Sinclair Mantell

Reprinted from the General Programme of the Savoyard Celebration Dinner, by kind permission of Mr. Carl Hentschel.

MR. COURTICE POUNDS.

"Be happy all – the feast is spread before ye;
Fear nothing, but enjoy yourselves, I pray!
Eat, aye, and drink – be merry, I implore ye,
For once let thoughtless folly rule the day."

1836–1911

Supper with Sullivan

"... the melodies are all as fresh as last year's wine and as exhilarating as sparkling champagne."

National Press

1, QUEEN'S MANSIONS,
June 7th, 1885.

Programme.

MUSIC.

MADAME ALBANI.
MDM. ANTOINETTE STERLING.
MR. EDWARD LLOYD.
SIGNOR CARPI.

TRIO . . "Three Little Maids,"
QUARTETT . "So please you, Sir,"
FROM

"THE MIKADO."

MISS LEONORA BRAHAM, MISS JESSIE BOND, MISS SYBIL GREY,
AND
MR. RUTLAND BARRINGTON.

After Supper a compressed version of the Musical Triumviretta,

"COX AND BOX."

MR. GEORGE GROSSMITH, MR. RUTLAND BARRINGTON,
AND
MR. ARTHUR CECIL.

As composer of the operas which were to become it's life-blood, Sir Arthur Sullivan had a close association with the D'Oyly Carte management, providing them with scores and orchestrations for all the collaborations with W.S. Gilbert, *Cox and Box*, much of *The Emerald Isle* (completed after his death by Edward German) and his grand opera *Ivanhoe*, written for the opening of Carte's Royal English Opera House in London. Between 1875 and 1899, Sullivan conducted performances by the D'Oyly Carte Company at the Royalty Theatre, Opera Comique, and the Savoy in London, the first ever *H.M.S Pinafore* and *The Pirates of Penzance* in the USA at the Fifth Avenue Theatre, New York, and the opening night of works with other librettists ... notably *Haddon Hall*, *The Chieftain*, *The Beauty Stone* and *The Rose of Persia*.

As a Director of the Savoy Hotel, Sullivan was a member of the Committee of Taste, advising the hotel management on recipes, wines and menus; an 1889 entry in his diary reminds him of an appointment *"to discuss kitchen affairs with Francois and Charpentier"*.

The programme, (*top left*), is for a dinner party held at Sullivan's home. It was attended by the Prince of Wales who finally went home at 3 am!

Clotilde Raquet

Clotilde Raquet was the Belgian kitchen maid employed in Sir Arthur Sullivan's service from 1885 to his death in 1900. The fiery Belgian became indispensable to him and progressed to the position of housekeeper, adviser and confidante at his London home.

Sullivan could hardly ignore her regular tantrums and he sacked her on at least one occasion ("*I don't think she thinks I mean it*"). She somehow managed to retain her job, offering up profuse apologies whenever she transgressed. Sir Arthur's diary implies she was in full flight while he tried to complete the composition of the Cachucha from *The Gondoliers*!

Along with his man-servant, Louis Jaeger, Clotilde was with Sullivan as he died and was generously remembered in his will.

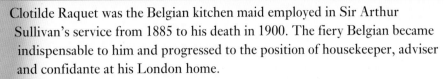

Sir Arthur Sullivan — Clotilde's Recipe

Shrimp or Prawn Kromeskys

Pound about a gill of Shrimps (picked from their shells of course, potted shrimps will do if the fresh ones are not to be had) in a mortar. Season with a little cayenne & a teaspoonful essence of shrimps, add a little cream & 2 raw yolks of eggs. Mix well. Melt a piece of butter about the size of an egg in a pan, stir in this the Shrimp mixture until thoroughly heated — Take it out of the pan & let it get quite cold. When cold it ought to be of the consistency of a soft smooth paste.

over.

Whip the white of the egg up separately & add it to the batter at the last moment.

The amount of butter & cream required will depend a good deal on the dryness of the Shrimps when pounded.

Take some thin strips of fat bacon about 1½ inch long & 2 wide, roll each strip of bacon round a portion of the prepared Shrimp paste. Dip each roll into the batter & fry all of them in boiling lard until they are of a pale golden colour.

The above quantities are for 8 people —

Batter

One raw yolk of egg, 1 Table spoonful flour, 1 ditto olive oil, 2 ditto cold milk & a little salt. Beat well up together.

Arthur Sullivan

1842–1900

D'Oyly's Haute Cuisine

Richard D'Oyly Carte (1844-1901) was the founder of the D'Oyly Carte Opera Company; the eldest of six children, he worked initially, for his father Richard Carte, in his music publishing firm – Rudall, Carte & Co. From there, he was able to publish many of his own compositions prior to establishing his own concert, operatic and lecture management agency where his many clients included Adelina Patti, Jacques Offenbach, Charles Gounod, George Grossmith and Oscar Wilde. In 1874, he leased the Opera Comique Theatre, producing French operettas but announcing his desire to "establish in London a permanent abode for light opera."

As Business Manager of the Royalty Theatre, he produced Gilbert & Sullivan's *Trial by Jury* in 1875 and thus began their long and enduring series of comic operas which were to gain their own home when Carte built the innovative Savoy Theatre, opening in October 1881. In 1884, work began on his most dazzling (and risky) project – the building of the Savoy Hotel, offering "shaded electric lights everywhere at all hours of night and day. No gas. Large and luxurious ascending rooms (lifts) running all night. Top floor rooms equal to the lowest. All the corridors warmed night and day. Seventy bathrooms."

César Ritz agreed to join the hotel as Manager (although only after visiting the finished building) and brought with him Louis Echenard as maître d'hôtel. With the appointment of Auguste Escoffier "Emperor of Cooks", Carte can claim to have brought Haute Cuisine to London.

His Royal English Opera House remains a landmark of the West End where, as the Palace Theatre, it remains a home for present day musicals under the ownership of Lord Lloyd Webber.

Pêches Melba

After a performance of *Lohengrin* at Covent Garden, the Duke of Orleans gave a dinner party at the Savoy to celebrate the success of Dame Nellie Melba. Escoffier created "Pêches Melba" in her honour and on this occasion, the dish was presented on a magnificent ice sculpture in the form of a swan, as featured in the opera, with piles of creamy vanilla ice cream placed between it's wings. In the kitchens, the peach halves had been gently poached in a vanilla syrup and flavoured with the zest of oranges and lemons. When cool, they were placed on the ice-cream, coated with a fresh raspberry sauce and sprinkled with toasted almonds. A gossamer effect was then created by adding a topping of spun sugar.

RICHARD D'OYLY CARTE
1844 - 1901

SAVOY HOTEL, LONDON.
THE PERFECTION OF LUXURY AND COMFORT.
THE RESTAURANT
Open to the Public
THE ONLY OPEN-AIR RESTAURANT IN LONDON

SOUPER DU 30 OCTOBRE, 1895.
MENU

Consommé Poule-au-Pot
Consommé de Tortue au Madère
-o-
Huîtres Favorite
-o-
Cailles Pochées à la Richelieu
-o-
Noisettes d'Agneau Fines Herbes
-o-
Brochette d'Ortolans
-o-
Suprême de Volaille Jeannette
-o-
Parfait de Foie-Gras
Salade Mignonne
-o-
Timbale d'Ecrevisses Américaine
Asperges Nouvelles
Biscuits Glacés
-o-
Bénédictins Rosé
Friandises
Fruits

SAVOY HOTEL.

"The Chef of Kings and the King of Chefs" was born in Villeneuve-Loubet in 1846. In 1890, he took over the kitchens at the Savoy and along with Ritz and his maître d'hôtel, Louis Echenard, he hired French cooks, reorganised the kitchens, created the "brigade" system, new sanitation standards, and developed awareness of the nutritional benefits of good, wholesome food properly prepared and served. Haute Cuisine had arrived and the Savoy, under his leadership, enjoyed immediate success with a distinguished clientele which included the Royal Family and dignitaries from around the world. His many friends and acquaintances included Sir Arthur Sullivan and George Grossmith.

La bonne cuisine est la base du véritable bonheur

A. sio

Mai 1911

Of his many creations, amongst the best known were Pêche Melba, Melba Toast, Bombe Nero, Fraises à la Sarah Bernhardt and, most importantly – the five "mother" sauces ... Béchamel, Velouté, Espagnole, Tomato and Hollandaise. His landmark book *The Complete Guide to the Art of Modern Cookery* is still in publication today.

Escoffier died in Monte Carlo in 1935.

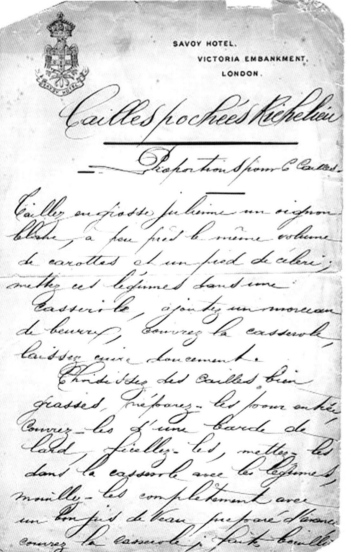

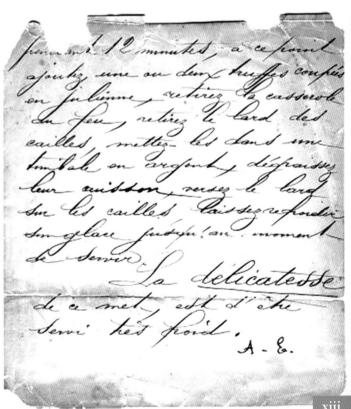

Ladles full of Love

J.M. Gordon

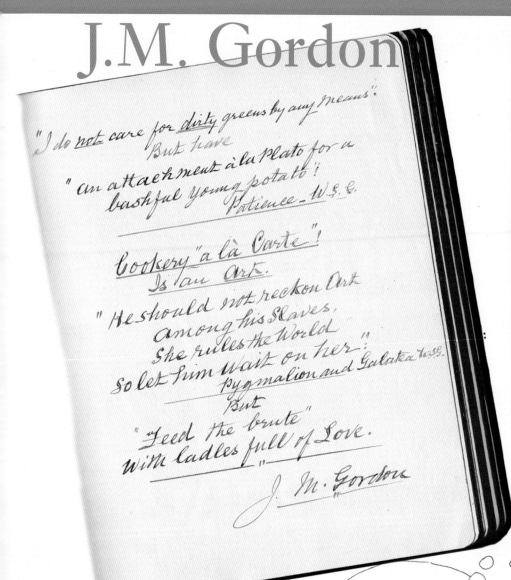

"I do not care for <u>dirty</u> greens by any means".
But have
"an attachment à la Plato for a
bashful young potato".
    Patience — W.S.G.

<u>Cookery "a là Carte"</u>!
    Is an Art.

"He should not reckon Art
    among his Slaves,
    She rules the World
So let him Wait on her."
    Pygmalion and Galatea W.S.G.
        But
"Feed the brute"
With ladles full of Love.
"
            J. M. Gordon

J.M.G. keeps order in the
recording studio!

Born in 1857, he toured in *Patience* for Richard D'Oyly Carte, prior to appearing in curtain-raisers at the Savoy and the premiere of *The Gondoliers* in 1889. He continued to tour for the Company and on the death of W.S. Gilbert was appointed Resident Stage Manager for the D'Oyly Carte Organization, a position he held for 28 years. He knew and understood the author's intentions and was dedicated to upholding them; he was also open to change and was responsible for the *Ruddigore* revisions made in 1921 and the Savoy Edition of *Cox & Box* which enabled the Company to use it in a double-bill with *The Sorcerer*. He retired in 1939 and died in Brighton in 1944.

The Selkirk Grace

Robert Wilson

"THE SELKIRK GRACE"
ROBERT BURNS.
1792.

SOME HA'E MEAT, AND CANNA EAT,
AND SOME WAD EAT THAT WANT IT;
BUT WEE HA'E MEAT, AND WE CAN EAT,
AND SAE THE LORD BE THANKIT.

Bob Wilson

TRIAL BY JURY

Written by W. S. GILBERT   Composed by ARTHUR SULLIVAN

The Learned Judge .... SYDNEY GRANVILLE
Counsel for the Plaintiff .... LESLIE RANDS
The Defendant .... ROBERT WILSON
Foreman of the Jury .... T. PENRY HUGHES
Usher .... RICHARD WALKER
Associate .... C. WILLIAM MORGAN
The Plaintiff .... ANN DRUMMOND-GRANT
First Bridesmaid .... KATHLEEN NAYLOR

Chorus of Jurymen, Bridesmaids and Public.

SCENE—A Court of Justice.

Followed by

THE PIRATES OF PENZANCE
or, The Slave of Duty

Written by W. S. GILBERT   Composed by ARTHUR SULLIVAN

Major-General Stanley .... MARTYN GREEN
The Pirate King .... DARRELL FANCOURT
Samuel (His Lieutenant) .... RICHARD WALKER
Frederic (the Pirate Apprentice) .... DEREK OLDHAM
Sergeant of Police .... SYDNEY GRANVILLE
Mabel .... BRENDA BENNETT
Edith .... ⎫   MARJORIE EYRE
Kate .... ⎬ (General Stanley's Daughters) ELIZABETH NICKELL-LEAN
Isabel .... ⎭   KATHLEEN NAYLOR
Ruth (Pirate Maid of All Work) .... EVELYN GARDINER

Chorus of Pirates, Police and General Stanley's Daughters.

ACT I .... A Rocky Seashore on the Coast of Cornwall
ACT II .... A Ruined Chapel, by Moonlight

Orchestra under the direction of ISIDORE GODFREY.

Interval of 10 Minutes between "Trial by Jury" and "The Pirates of Penzance."
Interval of 15 Minutes between the Acts of "The Pirates of Penzance."

Books of Words may be obtained from the Attendants, Price 1/-.

Born in Cambuslang, Scotland, in 1907, Robert Wilson studied in Glasgow prior to joining the D'Oyly Carte in 1931 as a chorister and understudy. He was soon making regular appearances as the Defendant in *Trial by Jury* – the one role he retained throughout his time with the Company. From 1935, he became a Co-Principal Tenor, sharing roles with Charles Goulding and John Dean, only to be demoted on the return of Derek Oldham; he was left with Francesco in *The Gondoliers*, Leonard Meryll in *The Yeomen of the Guard* and Defendant.

It was no surprise when he left in 1937 to rebuild his career; this he did rather successfully and became one of Scotland's top variety stars with an exclusive HMV recording contract, concert tours and numerous radio and television appearances including the famous White Heather Club.

He died in Ayr in 1964.

Sidney Pointer as Cyril in
Princess Ida

COCKTAILS

Lady Gilbert

Lucy Agnes Blois Turner married W.S. Gilbert in 1867; "Kitten" became Lady Gilbert when her husband was knighted by King Edward VII in 1907. In their social circle, they often held dinner parties with Lucy providing recipes from her personal collection.

These were carefully noted in her book of "Home Dinners" and include such specialities as Consommé aux Profiteroles, Filet Jardinière, Quail Soufflé and Escalopes de Saumon a là Windsor.

In 1914, she published her own *Kitty's Cookery Book* and the many recipes it contained certainly appeared to reflect the life she had enjoyed with her husband. These included Jenny Lind Soup, Sally Luns (*The Sorcerer*) and Rusks (*The Gondoliers*). Other, more unusual, dishes were Lady Abbess Tarts and Religious Cod!!

She also supervised and designed the landscaping of the grounds and gardens at their home in Middlesex – Grim's Dyke.

Lady Gilbert's New Year's Eve Milk Punch

Boil 1 quart of milk with the peel of 1 lemon thinly pared, 1
nutmeg, 2 blades of mace.

Have ready the yolks of two or three eggs mixed with a little cold
milk; pour the boiling milk on to it; then return it to the stew pan.

Make quite hot, but do not boil, stirring all the time.

Then put it in a jug or basin; add two wine glasses of rum,
1 tot of brandy and not quite a glass of Noyeau and sweeten to taste.

"A Thing of Beauty is a Joy forever,
Especially a Cook who's clean and clever."

Lady Gilbert
sketched by her husband

Sir Henry Lytton

"Knight of all he Savoyed"

"We shall never forget you; we honour the artist, we love the man. God bless you.

Yours, in gratitude and sincerity,

Stanley Baldwin.
Prime Minister"

Sir Henry Lytton was born on 3 January 1865 and spent a remarkable 50 years with D'Oyly Carte; he married Louie Henri in 1884 and, in his early days, appeared in Gilbert and Sullivan's original production of *Ruddygore* and, albeit with his own ideas of interpretation, understudied George Grossmith, creator of many of the "patter" roles. As Jack Point in *The Yeomen of the Guard*, Lytton's character died of a broken heart, unlike in the comic finale favoured by Grossmith, and it was as the travelling jester that he gave his final performance in 1934 aged 69! In 1931, whilst driving to Cambridge with his co-star Bertha Lewis, he had a serious car accident; the BBC issued regular progress reports on his condition and Bertha Lewis died from her injuries five days later.

In a varied career, he had also been an impressario and appeared in music hall, musical comedy (including a long West End run of *The Earl and the Girl* with a cast including numerous D'Oyly Carte Savoyards) and in pantomime in which he made his farewell to the stage at the Prince of Wales Theatre, Birmingham in 1935. Sir Henry Lytton died on 15 August 1936.

"There have been many who have made great reputations in the Gilbert and Sullivan characters, and when the roll comes to be written, Henry Lytton will undoubtedly be assigned a foremost place. He has played a wide variety of the parts, and the scope and versatility of his work is unique."

Rupert D'Oyly Carte

4

"Glad Eyes"

Early D'Oyly days :
Guiseppe in *The Gondoliers*

"Glad Eyes" (Lyttons special)

The yolk of one egg
The juice of a Lemon
One glass of French Vermouth
One glass of Italian Vermouth
One Glass of Gordons Gin
One Table spoonful of "Fine Fruits"
a dash of Soda Water

Henry Lytton

Happy days
Yours very sincerely
Henry Lytton

The Sultan in
The Rose of Persia

5

Sydney Granville

Sydney "Granny" Granville was associated with the D'Oyly Carte Opera Company from 1907 to 1942 and during the course of his professional life appeared in musical comedy, pantomime at the London Palladium, opera with the Moody – Manners Opera Co., G&S in Australia for the J.C.Williamson management, *The Beggar's Opera* at the Lyric Hammersmith and the 1939 Technicolor film of *The Mikado*. He played every light baritone role in the D'Oyly Carte's repertoire before finally landing the heavier character parts on the retirement of Leo Sheffield in 1928. These he played until 1942. Apparently, he didn't waste his high notes while warming-up in the dressing room believing they were in short supply and should be conserved!

Lancashire born and bred, he died in Stockport in 1959 at the age of 79.

"Granny's" Top – Tip

(before drinking Sir Henry's "Glad Eyes" cocktails!)

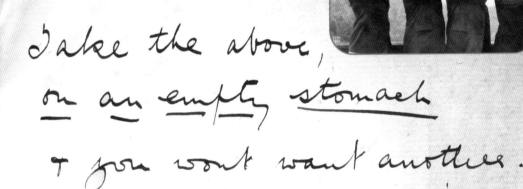

"Tantantara" with colleagues at the Clifton suspension bridge

Take the above,
on an empty stomach
& you wont want another.

Sydney Granville

Backstage with Martyn Green.
The Yeomen of the Guard

Brenda Bennett

Canadian Brenda Bennett was born in Winnipeg on 21 April 1914. After furthering her studies in London, she became Principal Soprano for D'Oyly Carte in 1936 staying for two years. She recorded the role of Yum-Yum in *The Mikado* and played Mabel, Phyllis, Rose Maybud, Lady Ella, Casilda, and later on Gianetta. Brenda lived to within two weeks of her 100th birthday and had organized a champagne party to celebrate.

Elegant Champagne

Ingredients

3 tbsp Crème de Cassis

Chilled Bottle of Champagne

Raspberries

Method

Pour the Crème de Cassis into champagne flutes

Share the champagne amongst the flutes

Drop a few raspberries into each glass

Serve

Toast Her Majesty the Queen and Gilbert & Sullivan, Drink!!

Brenda with Melvyn Tarran
at Oak Hall, Sussex

Front row, left to right: Jane Martin who starred in the J.C.Williamson G&S
productions in Australia, Cynthia Morey, Brenda and Jennifer Toye.
The gentlemen are Cynthia's husband, Tony Jennings (left) and John Fryatt (right).

Frederick Hobbs

Frederick Hobbs was a New Zealander and made his British debut with the Carl Rosa Opera Company and in musical comedy. He spent six years with the D'Oyly Carte playing most of the bass-baritone roles until the engagement of Darrell Fancourt. Back in Australia he played in G&S with the J.C. Williamson Company before rejoining D'Oyly Carte as Stage Manager then Business Manager. He died during the 1942 tour.

"White Lady"

One quarter lemon juice, one quarter Cointreau, and one half dry gin. Shake & strain into cocktail glass.

White Lady Cocktail

one quarter lemon juice, one quarter Cointreau, and one half dry Gin, shake & strain into cocktail glass.

Frederick Hobbs

Darrell Fancourt O.B.E.

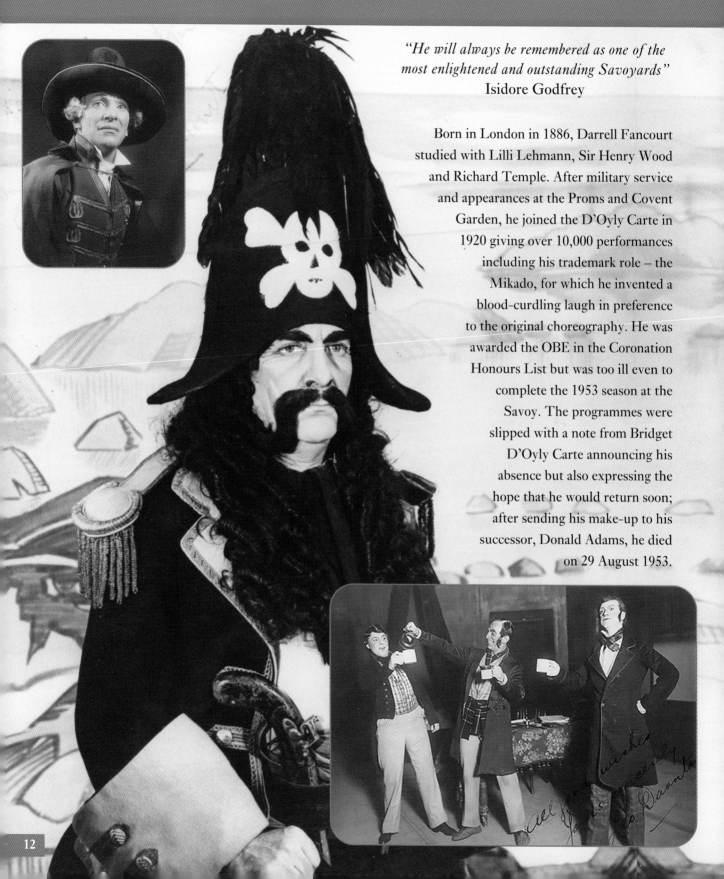

"He will always be remembered as one of the most enlightened and outstanding Savoyards"
Isidore Godfrey

Born in London in 1886, Darrell Fancourt studied with Lilli Lehmann, Sir Henry Wood and Richard Temple. After military service and appearances at the Proms and Covent Garden, he joined the D'Oyly Carte in 1920 giving over 10,000 performances including his trademark role – the Mikado, for which he invented a blood-curdling laugh in preference to the original choreography. He was awarded the OBE in the Coronation Honours List but was too ill even to complete the 1953 season at the Savoy. The programmes were slipped with a note from Bridget D'Oyly Carte announcing his absence but also expressing the hope that he would return soon; after sending his make-up to his successor, Donald Adams, he died on 29 August 1953.

Darrell demonstrates the Silver Streak effect . . .

"Silver Streak Cocktail"
Three equal parts of gin,
lemon juice, & cointreau, with
a dash of absinthe.

Darrell Fancourt.

Golf with Martyn Green

Isidore Godfrey O.B.E.

The "governor" of Gilbert and Sullivan conductors was born on 27 September 1900, joined D'Oyly Carte's small "New" Company in 1925 as accompanist, moved to the main Opera Company as Assistant Musical Director and Chorus Master in 1926 and was Musical Director from 1929-1968.

"There's something about those scores – some touch of genius – that makes that music live. One doesn't tire of it. It's a combination of the popular type of music which catches the ear immediately and the other kind, the classical, which requires study for appreciation; and Sullivan was fortunate in having Gilbert – a librettist whose work was perfectly suited to the mood of the music."
I.G.

"His sustained enthusiasm and freshness of approach cannot always have been easy, and the standard he set, his patience, good humour and affectionate loyalty fill me with admiration and sincerest gratitude."

Bridget D'Oyly Carte.

"Satan's Whisker"

"Satan's Whisker" Cocktail.

Gin, Italian Vermouth, French Vermouth, orange juice (fresh)

Two Parts each:

Orange curaçao - One part.

Perhaps a little less French, according to taste. This makes a smooth & deceptive cocktail.

"Goddie" with his wife Mary at the Millstream Restaurant, Bosham

The music quoted is from *Princess Ida* ...
"we've tried it, and we know, alas – we've tried it, and we know."

15

Elsie Winston

Elsie Winston sang with the chorus of the D'Oyly Carte New Opera Company from 1925-27 transferring to the D'Oyly Carte Opera Company in October of 1927 where she occasionally appeared as Pitti-Sing, Vittoria and Leila.

Miss Carte's Young Ladies 1971

A Special *Sorcerer* Cocktail

The **SORCERER** COCKTAIL

Specially created by
ARMANDO Head Bartender.
PLAZA BAR, HOTEL PICCADILLY.
MANCHESTER

Magical Ingredients

BELLS WHISKY ⅓
BLUE CURACAO ⅓
BENEDICTINE ⅓
GRENADINE

Fresh Orange Juice
to taste.

16

Cider Cup

Cider Cup.

Put 1 pint dry Cider into a
glass jug, add 1 tablespoonful
brandy, + 2 tablespoonfuls
of Orange wine, give it a
stir, add 1 orange, 1 apple,
slice'd, some sliced cucumber,
+ a sprig of borage (if obtainable)
stand the jug on ice, when
serving at last minute, add
some bits of ice, pour on it
some iced soda-water.

Elsie Winston

The D'Oyly Carte Opera Co. 1963

The "Witch's Curse" — a *Ruddigore* Cocktail

Created by Booth's Gin for our production of *Ruddigore* in the
1963/4 London season at the Savoy. A Launch was
originally planned in the Savoy Cocktail Bar with

Donald Adams   *Sir Roderic Murgatroyd*
John Reed   *Robin Oakapple*
Gillian Knight   *Dame Hannah*

But this was delayed and the whole Company was invited to
the distillery to learn about GIN!!
What a day.
The cocktail was really an alternative to a Bloody Mary.
Gin, Tomato Juice, Tabasco, Worcester Sauce, Salt and
Pepper. Down in one — oops!!!
Recipe supplied by:

*Miss Carte's Young Ladies 1963-1964 Savoy Theatre, London
(under the supervision of Miss Abby Hadfield.)*

17

Ella Halman

Dorothy Gill

"Turbot is ambitious brill"

Little Buttercup H.M.S. Pinafore

Patricia
Leonard

Christene Palmer

18

Peter Pratt

Beti Lloyd Jones

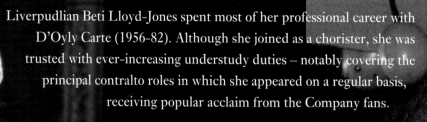

Liverpudlian Beti Lloyd-Jones spent most of her professional career with D'Oyly Carte (1956-82). Although she joined as a chorister, she was trusted with ever-increasing understudy duties – notably covering the principal contralto roles in which she appeared on a regular basis, receiving popular acclaim from the Company fans.

For some time she was cast as Lady Saphir in *Patience* (which she also recorded for Decca) but is best remembered for her portrayal of Inez in *The Gondoliers* and Mrs Partlet in *The Sorcerer* as well as Salata in *Utopia Ltd* and Bertha in *The Grand Duke*.

Over the years, Beti became a font of knowledge to many new choristers and was the "adopted stage mum" of John Reed – 'tho, as the accompanying fancy dress photograph illustrates, her influence over her "son" was somewhat liberal!

She eventually married Gordon (Mike) Mackenzie (ex chorister and Company Manager with the D'Oyly Carte) and they lived happily in Mike's native Scotland.

Mike had also enjoyed a successful career with the *White Heather Group*, recording duets with Robert Wilson and many Scottish songs as a solo artiste. After his death in 1995, Beti remained in Scotland for the rest of her life. She died in March 2014.

Ambitious Brill

Serves 4

Ingredients

700g Fresh Brill (filleted and skinned)
259g Mixed Wild Mushrooms
Red Onion ... medium diced
About 20 cherry tomatoes
3 cloves of garlic (chopped);
small bunch of flat-leafed parsley;
Salt and Black Pepper; Olive Oil; Soy Sauce

"Climbing over rocky mountain ..."

Method

Heat the oven to 180 degrees C.
Place the fillets in a lightly-greased baking tray; brush with olive oil and season with salt and pepper.
Cook the diced onion in a frying pan with olive oil for around 5 minutes; don't allow to brown.
Place the Brill in the oven for 12 minutes.
Clean the mushrooms and add, with the garlic, to the onions. Stir from time to time for 5 minutes. Towards the end of this, add the tomatoes and Soy sauce; taste and adjust seasoning if required.
At the last moment, add the parsley and stir it in.
Warm the plates, serve the sauce and put the Brill on top.
Serve with bread, salad or best of all – CHIPS!!!

Yours aye.
Beti x

Beti (centre) with (L) Jo Riordan (R) Jean Hindmarsh and, in the foreground, James Marsland

21

Helen Gilliland

Speaking in 1941: "*Cheek got me my first part. I was studying at the Royal College of Music in London. I stole out of the college and presented myself for an audition with Rupert D'Oyly Carte. Actually, I had been brought up very strictly in Ireland and the Gilbert and Sullivan operas were the only entertainments I had been allowed to see. I started with the Company right away and sang the leading prima donna roles.*"

Helen described herself as having a "*freak voice . . . I could manage The Magic Flute with ease*" and so impressed was Rupert D'Oyly Carte that she was invited to rejoin the Company for the return to London at the Princes Theatre in 1919 and again in 1921–22. She had been only the second recipient of the 'Gold Medal of All Ireland' (the first was John McCormack) and went on to appear in the West End and in New York including Revues with George Robey, *Stop Fooling* with Fred Astaire, Principal Boy in Pantomime, *Song of the Drum* (written especially for her) at Drury Lane and was offered a co-starring role with Maurice Chevalier in *The Love Parade*.

On 21 December 1942, *The Times* reported:

MISS HELEN GILLILAND MISSING AT SEA

From our own correspondent Bombay, December 20th

Miss Helen Gilliland, the actress, is missing after the torpedoeing of the ship in which she was travelling with her husband, Mr Peter Franklin. They left the ship together, but Mr Franklin was washed back into the ship and temporarily trapped. When he recovered, his wife could not be found in the darkness. The star of numerous London and New York successes, Miss Gilliland toured the Empire entertaining troops, and raised nearly £200,000 for war funds. She had just spent a year in India.

Potted Redherring

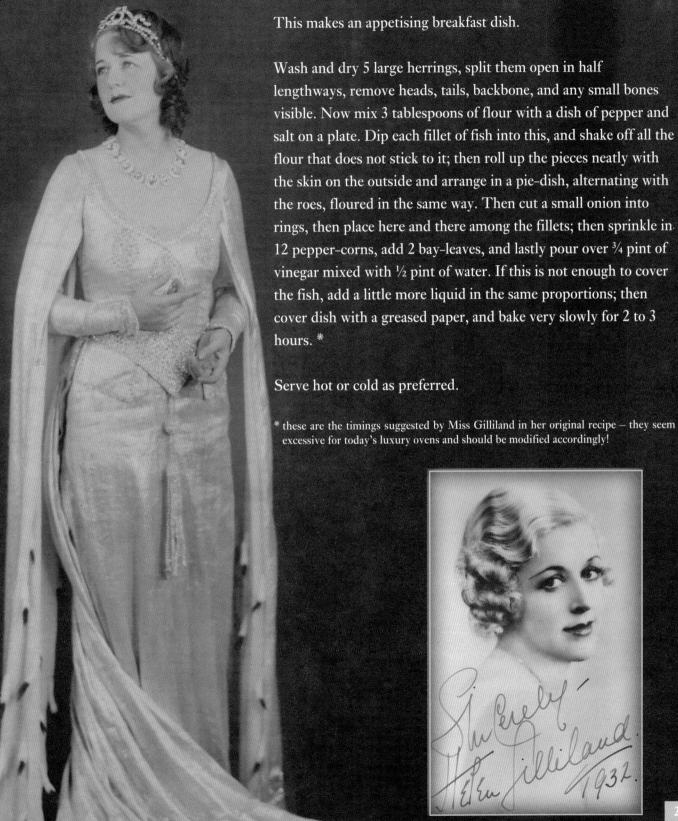

This makes an appetising breakfast dish.

Wash and dry 5 large herrings, split them open in half lengthways, remove heads, tails, backbone, and any small bones visible. Now mix 3 tablespoons of flour with a dish of pepper and salt on a plate. Dip each fillet of fish into this, and shake off all the flour that does not stick to it; then roll up the pieces neatly with the skin on the outside and arrange in a pie-dish, alternating with the roes, floured in the same way. Then cut a small onion into rings, then place here and there among the fillets; then sprinkle in 12 pepper-corns, add 2 bay-leaves, and lastly pour over ¾ pint of vinegar mixed with ½ pint of water. If this is not enough to cover the fish, add a little more liquid in the same proportions; then cover dish with a greased paper, and bake very slowly for 2 to 3 hours. *

Serve hot or cold as preferred.

* these are the timings suggested by Miss Gilliland in her original recipe – they seem excessive for today's luxury ovens and should be modified accordingly!

Roberta Morrell

Robbie is from West Bromwich and, after training at the Birmingham School of Music and the Royal College of Music, joined the D'Oyly Carte chorus in 1972, understudying and appearing occasionally as Inez, Kate (*Pirates*) and Hebe. From 1978 she played Hebe, Kate and Peep-Bo in her own right and also appeared in a segment from *The Mikado* in the film *Chariots of Fire*. After ten years in the Company, she carved out a highly successful career as a Director both at home and in America; this has included *The Magic of G&S* and several seasons at Gawsworth Summer Opera. She has worked tirelessly as an adjudicator and drama coach whilst her work as a writer includes a biography of the veteran Savoyard Kenneth Sandford and a murder mystery, *Vengeance Dire*!

Sgt. Morrell's Tangy Fish Pâté

... one of our more glamorous gigs with Valerie, Gareth, Roberta, Pat and Geoffrey

Ingredients

1 pack of boil in the bag kippers

100g Philadelphia cream cheese

1 small garlic clove, finely crushed

Juice of one lemon

Freshly ground black pepper

Lemon slices to garnish

Method

Cook the kippers following the advice on the packet.

Allow them to cool then place in a bowl, removing the skin and any large bones.

Mash the kippers with a fork, then add the cream cheese, garlic, lemon juice and a little freshly-ground pepper.

Thoroughly beat the ingredients together, then spoon into individual ramekins, or one serving dish if preferred.

Garnish each ramekin with a lemon slice.

Chill in the fridge for two hours.

Serve with melba toast or, better still, oat cakes.

with love from,

Roberta

Muriel Dickson

Muriel sang with the D'Oyly Carte from 1928–35. While appearing with the Company in New York she was spotted by the Director of the Metropolitan Opera and subsequently made her debut there in Smetana's *The Bartered Bride*. In her four-year stay at the Met, one of her many highlights was as Musetta in *La Bohème* with Jussi Bjorling. On her return to the UK, she was offered a contract at Covent Garden but opted to get married instead, later concentrating on a career as a singing teacher.

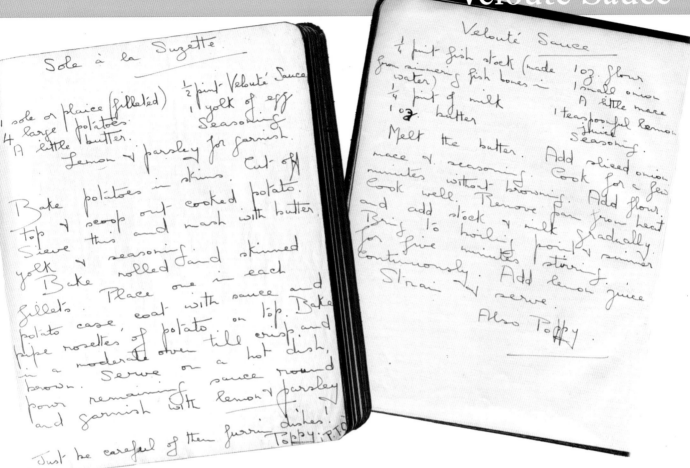

Sole à la Suzette

1 sole or plaice (filleted)   ½ pint Velouté Sauce
4 large potatoes   1 yolk of egg
A little butter   Seasoning
Lemon & parsley for garnish.

Cut off skins. Bake potatoes in skins. Cut off top & scoop out cooked potato. Sieve this and mash with butter, yolk & seasoning and skinned fillets. Bake rolled and skinned fillets. Place one in each potato case, coat with sauce and pipe rosettes of potato on top. Bake in a moderate oven till crisp and brown. Serve on a hot dish, pour remaining sauce round and garnish with lemon & parsley.
Toppy. P.T.O.

Just be careful of these furry dishes!

Velouté Sauce

¼ pint fish stock (made   1 oz flour
from simmering fish bones in   1 small onion
water)   A little mace
¼ pint of milk   1 teaspoonful lemon
1 oz butter   juice
                              Seasoning.

Melt the butter. Add sliced onion, mace & seasoning. Cook for a few minutes without browning. Add flour, cook well. Remove pan from heat and add stock & milk gradually. Bring to boiling point, simmer for five minutes, stirring continuously. Add lemon juice. Strain & serve.

Also Toppy

---

64   MUSICAL AMERICA for February 10, 1939

MURIEL DICKSON

"A RADIANT VOICE AND A WELCOME SIGHT" NEWSWEEK MAGAZINE

Scottish Soprano
Metropolitan Opera Association

THE DELIGHTFUL NEW CONCERT ATTRACTION

Warmly Greeted By The New York Press
Following Her Town Hall Recital, Dec. 14, 1938

● "A combination of lovely voice, intelligent singing, fine diction and excellent stage presence made Muriel Dickson's recital in Town Hall yesterday afternoon one of the season's outstanding concert debuts. Add to that her personal beauty and winning charm of manner and you have the story in a nutshell."—*World-Telegram*

● "Muriel Dickson, has not blushed unseen since her arrival here as a member of the D'Oyly Carte Opera Company some years ago. Her preeminence as a Savoyard was speedily established, and when she made the jump to the Metropolitan Opera she continued the good work with charming impersonations in 'The Bartered Bride' and 'Amelia Goes to the Ball.' But it needed her singing of a searching program yesterday to establish how fine an artist she really is.

"Miss Dickson sang with good taste, discrimination and intelligence. Each song was for her a poetic entity, to be realized with its special mood and flavor."—*Times*

"Princess Ida"

GILBERT AND SULLIVAN AT THE SAVOY

The Gilbert and Sullivan opera "Princess Ida" was effectively produced at the Savoy Theatre last night. It went through without a hitch, and except for a tendency on the part of the chorus to swallow a word or two and on the part of the orchestra to play rather loudly, all was as clear as a bell.

Of Sir Henry Lytton's King Gama there is naturally no need to say otherwise than that it was as lively and as fluent as are all his rôles. In those circumstances to say that Mr. Richard Watson's King Hildebrand was a worthy companion to Gama is in itself sufficient and high praise. But the palm must go to Miss Muriel Dickson, who gave us a Princess Ida played and sung with much grace and vigour. This singer's voice is alone worth going to the Savoy to hear in its delightful clarity of tone and natural unforced production.

Jennifer Toye

After studying in Florence under the tutorship of her uncle, Francis Toye, Jennifer joined the D'Oyly Carte in 1953 singing small roles and chorus.

Her steady progress through the ranks included successful appearances as the Plaintiff and Casilda – roles she would continue to play for her entire time in the Company. She was made a Principal in 1960, singing Elsie Maynard, Josephine, Mabel, Lady Ella and eventually Yum Yum and Lady Psyche. From time to time her duties would also include Kate in *The Yeomen of the Guard* and Celia in *Iolanthe*.

Jennifer was the voice of Zorah in the Halas and Batchelor cartoon of *Ruddigore*.

Her uncle, Geoffrey Toye, was the D'Oyly Carte Musical Director from 1919-24 and is remembered for his reworking of the *Ruddigore* Overture.

Jennifer (centre)
with Philip Potter and Jean Hindmarsh

Jennifer Toye

Tempura Prawns.

1 lb raw king prawns - defrosted if frozen.
(500g)
  50g plain flour
  25g corn flour
  Salt tsp.
100ml ice cold sparkling water.
  sunflower oil for frying.

——— * ———

Sift flours into a bowl, season then
gradually whisk in enough water to
make a batter the thickness of
double cream, taking care not to overwhisk.

Heat oil in wok or deep frying pan
To test add a cube of bread and it
should brown in 30 seconds.
Dip half of prawns in batter to coat
and lower into hot oil. Fry for 2-3
minutes until light golden + crisp.
Remove with slotted spoon and drain
on kitchen paper. Keep warm and
repeat with remaining prawns.
  Serve with mayonnaise (garlic if
preferred) or Chilli Dipping sauce.
  Serves 2-3
NB use peeled prawns - shells
  are a mess!

With all good
wishes
Jennifer Toye.

Jennifer Toye.

29

Lorraine Dulcie Daniels

After study at Trinity College, and winning the Elisabeth Schumann Lieder Competition, Lorraine joined the D'Oyly Carte Chorus in 1976 as an understudy. Within a year she was playing the smaller roles of Edith, Leila and Lady Saphir and took over as Principal Mezzo-Soprano for the 1979 tour of Australia and New Zealand. On return to the UK she added the roles of Tessa, Phoebe, Constance and subsequently Mad Margaret to her repertoire and remained with the Company until 27 February 1982; that night, she was a great success in her comedy work with Kenneth Sandford and throughout her time with D'Oyly Carte was much-admired for the pure clear tone of her fine voice, her striking looks and the warmth and charm of her performances.

She has continued to enjoy a flourishing concert career throughout the UK and North America.

Dulcie's Sweetcorn
& Prawn Chowder

Serves 4 – 6

Ingredients

1 325g can of sweet corn

600ml / 1 pint of milk

30g / 1oz of butter

I medium onion – thinly sliced

2 garlic cloves, crushed

1 red pepper, seeded and diced

1 celery stick, chopped

2 medium potatoes, diced

15 ml / 1 tbsp plain flour

300 ml / half a pint of fish stock (Can be made from a fish stock cube)

240g uncooked or cooked prawns (More prawns can be added)

1 teaspoon of ground turmeric

2 teaspoons of tarragon (more can be added)

150ml / quarter of a pint of single cream

Salt and Pepper (freshly ground black pepper is better)

Method

1. Melt the butter in a large saucepan and gently fry the onion and garlic until soft but not browned. Add the red pepper, celery and potatoes and heat for a further 3-4 minutes, stirring frequently. Do not allow the vegetables to brown.
2. Stir in the flour and then a little drop of the milk. Gradually add the fish stock and the rest of the milk. Season with salt, pepper, turmeric and tarragon.
3. Bring to the boil and then simmer, partially covered, for 15-20 minutes until the vegetables are tender.
4. Add the prawns and tin of sweetcorn and cook for 5 minutes.
5. Add the cream. Check the seasoning and serve with fresh crusty bread.

"This is a hearty soup that can be eaten as a meal in itself!!
One of our family favourites!"

Oliver White

Oliver graduated in music from Durham University and won a scholarship to study singing at the RCM. Performances include principal tenor with the D'Oyly Carte (West End), Carl Rosa (touring the USA, Canada and the UK), Opera Holland Park, Raymond Gubbay, Opera della Luna, Armonico Consort, and the National G&S Opera Company.

He has broadcast on Radio 2 (*Friday Night is Music Night*) Radio 3 and Classic FM, recorded for SkyArts TV, ITV and Chandos, appeared at The Proms, all the major concert halls and cathedrals of the UK and Ireland, and as soloist with the Philharmonia, RLPO and BSO, with conductors including Richard Hickox, John Wilson and David Hill. He is a visiting tutor at Chetham's School of Music, and was Director of Music at St Augustine's, Kensington for 12 years.

When not working, Oliver can be found riding the waves of the Atlantic, followed by sampling a pint of fine Cornish ale and spending the night in his vintage VW.

Fairfax's Fish Fingers

Fairfax's Fish Fingers

Makes around <u>20</u> (can be frozen when raw)

- 250g of pollack (or any firm-fleshed fish), skinned and deboned.
- 3 tbsp plain flour
- 2 eggs, lightly beaten.
- 100g breadcrumbs
- pinch of thyme
- pinch of cayenne pepper <u>OR</u> paprika
- ground black pepper and sea salt

- Cut the fish into chunks, not very thick.
- Season the flour on one plate (with the spices to your particular taste ...)
- Add the thyme to the breadcrumbs on another plate.

- With each piece of fish, in turn, dust it lightly in flour, avoiding excess, then dip in the beaten egg, again avoiding excess and finally coat in breadcrumbs, pressing them in with your fingers.

- Cook in oil in a frying pan until golden and crisp, and cooked through, and drain on kitchen paper. Medium heat is best.

HAPPY EATING!

Serve with a dip of your choosing!!.

Anne Sessions

Birmingham-born Anne Sessions was associated with the D'Oyly Carte from 1956-63 and 1965-69. During the intervening period she was in the West End production of *My Fair Lady*. She played many of the smaller soprano roles (Chloe, Guilia, Fiametta, Celia etc.) but was a Principal Soprano understudy to be reckoned with and played several roles during the absences of Mary Sansom and Jean Hindmarsh. These included Yum-Yum, Patience, Phyllis, Gianetta and Rose Maybud. From 1965, she appeared regularly as Lady Psyche in *Princess Ida*, Lady Ella in *Patience* and the Plaintiff in *Trial by Jury*. She remains active in the world of Gilbert and Sullivan and was Inez in *The Gondoliers* for the G&S Opera Company at the Buxton International Festival.

SMOKED FISH HASH:

1 Tablespn oil.
60g (2ozs) butter
4 Rashers streaky Bacon, halved.
300g - 400g (10 - 14ozs)
    Cook diced potatoes
300gs. (10 ozs) smoked Haddock
or smoked Mackerel fillet,
cut into bite sized chunks
    (check for bones)
4 spring onions
        trimmed & sliced
Salt & freshly ground black pepper.

method.
Heat the oil & half the butter in a large Pan.
Fry the bacon & potatoes until they are crispa brown
Push them to one side of the pan, and add the remaining
butter and the fish.

        Cook for a minute, then turn the fish over
& add the spring onions.
                Cook for a few minutes until the fish
is cooked & season well.

_____

This is a lovely supper dish! Bon appetit!

                        Sincerely
                        Anne Sessions.

35

Gillian Knight

In 1959, Gill joined the D'Oyly Carte, straight from the Royal Academy, as a temporary replacement for Ann Drummond Grant. When "Drummie" died, Gillian began a six year stay as Principal Contralto with the Company and a life-long association with the Gilbert and Sullivan Operas. It was clear to her many admirers that here was an artist destined for a very special career in music; at Sadler's Wells Opera her successes included Ragonde in *Count Ory*, Isabella in *The Italian Girl in Algiers* and Suzuki in *Madam Butterfly* and as a result of her portrayal of Carmen, she was invited to repeat the role at the Royal Opera House, taking over from Tatiana Troyanos and, subsequently, Grace Bumbry.

> **"There grew a little flower 'neath a great oak tree"**
> Dame Hannah
> *Ruddigore*

"Miss Knight conveyed more than any recent Carmen in this house, the sense of doom in Bizet's marvellous writing ... going to her end, like all the best Carmens, with an almost heroic insolence". The Times

This led to a thirty year association with Covent Garden, performances of the role opposite Placido Domingo and the start of an international career that would take her to Paris, Frankfurt, Basel, Chicago, Dallas and to every major British opera company. Her recording catalogue is equally extraordinary, working with the world's greatest conductors including Solti, Maazel, Colin Davis, Pierre Boulez and James Levine. When the D'Oyly Carte was revived in 1988, Gillian returned to Gilbert and Sullivan *"with more richness and energy than ever"* ... (Arthur Jacobs), reminding audiences of the possibility of class and finesse in the performance of the works.

It would be difficult to think of a more popular, respected and generous artist in the long history of the Savoy Operas.

Gill Knight's Fish Pie

2 portions Cod or Haddock
1 pack smoked Mackerel
1 tin salmon (medium, skinless & boneless)
2 handfuls frozen peas
½ pt. milk
1 level dessertspoon cornflour
handful flat leafed parsley
salt & pepper
Mashed potatoes & grated cheese

Poach the cod in the milk until flaky.
Meanwhile arrange mackerel, salmon & peas in a buttered dish, mixing together with cod.

Carefully (!) mix the cornflour into the milk from the poached fish and simmer for three minutes. Add the chopped parsley and season to taste. Mix into the fish.

Top with mashed potato & add grated cheese. Bake at 180° until nicely browned (about 20-25 mins)

Do try to enjoy it.

xx

Best wishes
Gillian Knight

Peter Pratt

Peter Pratt was born in Eastbourne in 1923 and joined the D'Oyly Carte Opera Company in 1945, soon becoming second understudy to Martyn Green. It was after a surprise appearance as Robin in *Ruddigore* that his fate was sealed and after a few seasons as principal understudy he took over the comedy roles in 1951. This also heralded his much-loved stage partnership with Ann Drummond – Grant, both of them growing in stature as the decade continued. Generally acknowledged as a superb actor by his colleagues, he began to scoop first class press reviews for his delivery, characterization, skill and under-stated style.

"He was bringing to his performances the sort of authority his two most famous twentieth century predecessors had brought to theirs"

Tony Joseph

He decided to leave the Company in 1959 and enjoyed a full career in television, radio and theatre (including *A Month in the Country* in the West End). He was a member of the BBC Repertory Company, and presented all 13 Savoy Operas on BBC Radio, playing the comedy roles in each. He returned to the D'Oyly Carte for the Centenary Season playing opposite Kenneth Sandford and John Ayldon in *Dramatic License* by William Douglas Home and wrote the television play *Jack Point*. In 1976, he played the Master in *Doctor Who*, again for the BBC.

He was married to Patience, the daughter of Leo Sheffield, and died in 1995.

Sea Bass with rosemary and sea-salt

Ingredients Serves 1

I sea bass fillet
Olive oil
I lemon (sliced)
4 sprigs of Rosemary
Sea-salt

Method

1. Preheat the oven to 220C / 440F / Gas mark 7.
2. Cut diagonally into the skin of the fish, exposing the flesh.
3. Put the rosemary into the flesh.
4. Rub the fish with olive oil.
5. Sprinkle with sea-salt.
6. Sear in a pan, skin down, until the skin crispens.
7. Transfer to the hot oven for 5 minutes.
8. Serve with fresh lemon and olive oil.

(Other favourite herbs, such as fresh thyme, may also be added.)

"Life's a pudding full of plums"

Peggy Ann Jones

Peggy Ann Jones joined the D'Oyly Carte aged 19 and rose to become one of its most memorable performers. Blessed with a rich mezzo-soprano voice and exceptional acting and comic skills she was unforgettable as Pitti-Sing, Mad Margaret, Phoebe Meryll and Mrs Partlet in the 1971 revival of *The Sorcerer*. She appeared in the film of *The Mikado* and on the soundtrack of the *Ruddigore* cartoon as well as giving brilliant stage performances as Lady Angela and the title role in *Iolanthe*. She was much missed when she left the Company but enjoyed a successful career in the West End (including *The Phantom of the Opera*, *Evita* and *Liza of Lambeth*) and in television, film and commercials.

Yeoman's Tuna Fish Pie

Together again with Kenneth Sandford 1993

Ingredients

Use tinned tuna in brine, drained.
1 Hard boiled egg – chopped up.
Grated cheese
8oz Mashed potatoes.
1 Egg beaten with a little milk

Method

Mix tuna and hard boiled egg into potato mash, with beaten egg
& season. Place in ovenproof dish & top with grated cheese.
Cook for 30 mins at 150°c (300°f, Gas mark 3)

Peggy Ann Jones

On tour in America
with Brue Worsley of
the D'Oyly Carte
management team

Barry Clark

Barry was a member of the D'Oyly Carte Opera Company from 1971–82.

He regularly played Franceso in *The Gondoliers* and First Yeoman in *The Yeomen of the Guard* but as Principal Tenor Understudy appeared in most of the leading roles including Alexis in *The Sorcerer* and Cyril in *Princess Ida*. For Decca, he recorded both Francesco and First Yeoman.

He sang with Scottish Opera and the New Sadler's Wells Opera and was in the original London cast of *The Phantom of the Opera* playing the Auctioneer, uttering the first words on the first night. His superb acting ability and comic timing proved invaluable when, in later years, he would play some of the G&S "patter" roles with the Carl Rosa Opera.

His play *Monarchs of All They Savoy* was premiered at the Player's Theatre, London.

Baz's Posh Fish 'n' Chips

Ingredients:

To serve 2. Two large fillets of fish, e.g.; haddock or cod, but any good solid fish will do.
Dried dill
Tbs olive oil + a little unsalted butter
Milled black pepper/sea salt
Three medium potatoes
One large red onion
One clove garlic (crushed)
One tin mushy peas
One egg
Fresh parsley to garnish

On tour for the Concordia Foundation with Patricia Leonard, Tania Whatley and Alan Watt.

Method:

Preheat oven to 180°c. Put small pan of water on to boil while oven heats.
Season & sprinkle dried dill on fish. Arrange fish on foil lined baking tray & drizzle on some oil & a knob of butter.
Bake for 25-30 mins depending on type of oven. Place fish towards top but not right at the top of the oven.
Meanwhile peel & cut potatoes into chunks & parboil them for 5-7 mins.
Drain potatoes & mash, adding yolk & white of the egg + seasoning.
Sauté the onions & garlic (cook onions 'til transparent) & add to potato mixture. In the same frying pan as you sautéed the onions, now put the potatoes mixture, add a bit more oil/butter if necessary & cook the potatoes steadily, forming them into four small cakes. Turn them over regulary 'til cooked through & golden brown on both sides.
While you are sautéing the potatoes, gently heat the mushy peas in a separate saucepan – taking care not to boil them.
Cook on fish & when golden brown & cooked through, arrange on bed of mushy peas, check seasoning, & put two potato cakes either side.
Garnish with parsley & serve.

"A good, robust New Zealand Sauvignon Blanc goes well with this, particularly during the cooking process.
Eat hearty!"

"There's lots of good fish in the sea"
Best wishes,
Barry Clarke

Linda Anne Hutchison

Linda first sang Gilbert
and Sullivan at
Gordonstoun School before
studying at the Guildhall
School of Music where she won
the Sydney de Vries Opera Prize.
As a finalist in the Kathleen Ferrier
Scholarship Competition, she came to
the notice of the D'Oyly Carte management and
was offered a contract in 1969. After only one year in the
chorus and as an understudy, she was made Principal
Soprano and over the following three years was memorable
as Elsie in *The Yeomen of the Guard*, Phyllis in *Iolanthe*,
Constance in *The Sorcerer* and her other roles – Gianetta,
Josephine and Patience. Since leaving the Company in 1973,
Linda has enjoyed a hugely successful career in teaching at the
Royal Scottish Academy, Birkbeck College, the Irish College of
Music Theatre and the Guildhall School of Music and Drama,
where her story began.

Salmon

with Bacon and Tarragon

Ingredients

4 salmon fillets (preferably Scottish)
1 small, finely chopped onion
2 slices of thin bacon, diced
3 oz/90g butter
Quarter teaspoon dried tarragon
2 tablespoons lemon juice
Large sheet of buttered kitchen foil
Double cream or crème fraiche

Method

Pre-heat the oven to 400F (200C or Gas Mark 6). Fry the finely chopped onion in butter in a pan until soft and golden (but not burnt). Add the bacon and tarragon and cook for another two minutes; then stir in the lemon juice.

Put a large piece of buttered kitchen foil on a baking sheet or in an ovenproof dish, place the salmon fillets on this and cover with the onion and bacon mixture. Fold over the foil and seal to make a parcel. Bake for 15-20 minutes.

Serve with a tablespoon of thick cream or crème fraiche and fresh vegetables.

"Quantities need not be exact. I have a wonderful local butcher
and I buy the 'eye' of bacon from him.
I usually put in lots of bacon and a generous dose of tarragon."

Linda A Hutchison

Frances McCafferty

Engagements with the D'Oyly Carte Opera Company marked the beginning of a successful and varied operatic career for Frances. She played Juno in *Orpheus in the Underworld*, Kate in *The Pirates of Penzance*, Little Buttercup in *H.M.S. Pinafore,* Katisha in *The Mikado* and sang Lady Angela in the Company's last recording of *Patience*. Her association with Sullivan's music continued with TER recordings of *H.M.S. Pinafore* and *Sullivan & Co.*

Her many appearances at the Royal Opera House, Covent Garden, have included the world premier of *Sophie's Choice*, *The Rake's Progress*, *Elektra*, *Lulu* and *Boris Godunov* whilst at the English National Opera, she has sung Mistress Quickly in *Falstaff* and Katisha in the Jonathan Miller production of *The Mikado*. Frances has graced the stages of Glyndebourne, Opera North, Scottish Opera and many of the European Companies while maintaining an impressive concert career with all of the major UK Symphony Orchestras and further appearances in the Gilbert and Sullivan Operas.

or The Dame's Tower

125g CHILLED BUTTER, CUBED
125g PLAIN FLOUR
25g FRESHLY GRATED PARMESAN
SALT AND FRESH GROUND BLACK PEPPER
LARGE PINCH OF CAYENNE PEPPER

PREHEAT OVEN TO 180C / 350F / GAS MARK 4

RUB BUTTER INTO FLOUR TO ACHIEVE THE APPEARANCE OF FINE BREADCRUMBS
STIR IN ALL OTHER INGREDIENTS AND WORK TOGETHER INTO A BALL
TURN OUT ONTO LIGHTLY FLOURED BOARD AND KNEAD UNTIL SMOOTH.

FLATTEN BALL OF DOUGH SLIGHTLY AND ROLL OUT BETWEEN TWO SHEETS OF CLING FILM.
REMOVE FILM AND CUT OUT ROUNDS APPROX 7.CM = 10-12 ROUNDS.
CAREFULLY TRANSFER TO A LIGHTLY BUTTERED BAKING SHEET. BAKE IN THE
CENTRE OF THE OVEN FOR 12-15 MINUTES UNTIL GOLDEN BROWN. REMOVE
FROM OVEN AND LEAVE TO COOL ON SHEET.

MEANWHILE, WHIP TOGETHER 150 ML WHIPPING CREAM, 2 x 5ml SPLEMON JUICE
AND SEASONING (SALT - PEPPER) UNTIL IT FORMS PEAKS. STIR IN 3 x 15 ML SP.
CHOPPED FRESH CHIVES.

SPOON A LITTLE CREAM ONTO A BISCUIT & COVER WITH SMOKED SALMON. REPEAT
THIS PROCESS TO BUILD A TOWER — x3 IS USUALLY SUFFICIENT.
SERVE GARNISHED WITH A LEMON WEDGE AND SOME WHOLE CHIVES.

Best Wishes and Bon Apetit!

Frances McCafferty.

"Katisha" has taken off her wig and enjoys
an interval chat and light refreshment with
Musical Director John Owen Edwards

Ken Robertson-Scott

Ken joined the D'Oyly Carte stage management team in 1975 (the Centenary year), and during his five seasons with them toured twice to the USA and Canada and in 1976, Australia and New Zealand.

On leaving the Company, Ken spent twenty years with the BBC and now continues to work on productions of the Gilbert and Sullivan operas in the USA and at home.

A 1950s impression of the D'Oyly Carte Prompt Corner!

Ken's Salmon Plait

Ingredients

1. 8 oz puff pastry
2. 1lb poached Salmon
3. ¼ pint Béchamel Sauce
4. ½ small cucumber deseeded not peeled
5. 1 table spoon chopped parsley
6. Mace
7. Egg Wash

Method

Roll out pastry thinly into rectangle. Leave to rest while preparing the filling.

Flake Salmon, remove skin, bones and any nasty things. Mix with parsley and Béchamel sauce.

Chop the cucumber into ¼ inch bits and put layer of cucumber down the centre of pastry.

Top with Salmon mixture and dust lightly with mace; cut diagonal slits at ½ intervals in pastry on either side up to the filling.

Brush down outer edges; with egg wash, and fold over filling taking a strip from either side.

Brush with egg wash being careful not to coat edges put in cool place to rest.

Bake in hot oven mark 7 until well risen and golden brown – about 30 mins.

Serve hot with new pots peas etc.

Reunited with Ken Sandford and John Reed at the International G&S Festival

Jill Pert

After graduating from the University of Toronto, Jill continued her studies at the London Opera Centre and after a short spell with the Canadian Opera Company, joined the D'Oyly Carte Opera Company in 1979 as understudy to Patricia Leonard. She stayed with the Company until the temporary closure in 1982 returning as a Principal Contralto with the New D'Oyly Carte Company from 1988–2002, appearing as the Duchess, Katisha, Queen of the Fairies, Ruth, Buttercup and Dame Carruthers. She also sang in the Company's production of *Orpheus in the Underworld* and a new recording of *Patience*.

Other notable work includes *The Sound of Music*, a season at Bristol Old Vic, Lady Blanche in Ken Russell's production of *Princess Ida* at the English National Opera and numerous appearances at the International G&S Festival with the Gilbert and Sullivan Opera Company.

Fish Bake

Ingredients

4 oz. Cod fillet.

4 oz. Smoked Haddock fillet.

4 oz. Salmon fillet

4 oz. Prawns (cooked and peeled)

2 oz. butter

2 oz. plain flour

Milk

Salt and black pepper, herbs of your choice - parsley, chives, dill.

1 lb. potatoes - peeled, cooked and mashed

2 oz. grated Cheddar cheese

... visiting Ella Halman in Penrith

Method

Poach the fish in 8 oz. of water until tender- about 10/15 minutes. Drain and reserve the liquor, making it up by adding the milk to ½ pint. Flake the fish, removing any skins.

In a saucepan, and over a low heat, melt the butter, and then stir in the flour to make a paste. Gradually add the liquor mixture, stirring continually to avoid any lumps1 If it seems a little too thick, add a little more milk. Don't allow it to boil, but let it simmer for a moment or two (for quickness, a packet of white sauce can be substituted!) Season the sauce with salt, black pepper and your favourite herbs- fresh, if possible.

Stir in the flaked fish and the prawns, and cook gently for a few moments. Pour into an oven-proof dish. Top with the mashed potato and sprinkle the grated cheese over the top. Bake in a moderately hot oven for about 30 minutes or until lightly browned on top.

This dish can be made in advance and refrigerated overnight. However, if you do this, don't add the cheese until you bake it prior to serving.

The great thing about this recipe is that you can substitute different sorts of white fish, and use your favourite seasonings. You can also use different sorts of cheese for the topping- a mix of Cheddar and Double Gloucester is very pretty!

Jill with
John Reed

"I hope you enjoy it!"

(signature) x (PERT)

"Last Night"
antics in London ... the
D'Oyly Carte charladies

51

"Buon' giorno, signorine!"

The Gondoliers

Gondolieri e contadini . . .

A company press call from the 1950s with Bristol substituting for Venice.

Jean Hindmarsh as Gianetta in
The Gondoliers

P
A
S
T
A

53

Jean Hindmarsh

Without doubt, one of the finest sopranos in the D'Oyly Carte G&S world, Jean was runner-up in the first Kathleen Ferrier Competition where she was spotted by a member of the D'Oyly Carte management. In March 1956 she was engaged as Principal Soprano with immediate success and press recognition. Her recordings of Josephine in *H.M.S. Pinafore* and Mabel in *The Pirates of Penzance* (opposite Thomas Round) are world-class and one of her greatest stage triumphs was in the title role of Princess Ida. After leaving the Company in 1960, she returned many times over the following nine years as a Guest Artist, always remaining a favourite of Musical Director Isidore Godfrey. In more recent times, she has delighted audiences at the International G&S Festival – still singing "Minerva" quite beautifully.

Lasagne

Lasagne

1 lb minced beef
½ lb chopped onions
large tin tomatoes
¼ pint dry white wine
2 chicken stock cubes
2 cloves garlic
3 tablespoons tomato purée
2 teaspoons oregano

Cook all ingredients slowly for 1 hour

White sauce

1 large tablespoon plain flour
2 oz butter
Salt pepper punch nutmeg
1 pint milk

layers   mince
          lasagne
          mince
          lasagne
          Sauce
Sprinkle with parmesan
Cook 300° – approx ¾ hr till golden brown.

Method for the White Sauce
(suggested by Melvyn)

Melt the butter in a saucepan; add flour; cook for a short while, stirring continuously.
Gradually add the milk. Finish with salt, pepper and nutmeg.

Love Jean xx

Jean (centre) with Melvyn and
Kay Tarran

Christene Palmer

Christene Palmer was the D'Oyly Carte Principal Contralto from 1965-71. Born in Geelong, Australia, she trained in Melbourne and sang with the Elizabethan Opera Company before coming to England to continue her studies at the National School of Opera. After two seasons at Glyndebourne she made her debut with the D'Oyly Carte on the 1965 Spring Tour with immediate success. She also played Katisha in the film of *The Mikado* and appeared in the televised performance of *Patience* for the BBC. During this time she struck up a memorable stage partnership with John Reed and met her husband-to-be, chorister Norman Wright. *The Times* praised her "vintage" performance as Ruth in the '68 recording of *The Pirates of Penzance* and her many admirers appreciate her "Little Flower" duet with John Ayldon on the *Songs and Snatches* collection – full of character and tenderness. On stage, it was impossible to believe that the elderly Dame Hannah was being played by an artist barely in her thirties, and her portrayals will all be remembered for their energy and sincerity.

"Christene Palmer – domineering in Mikado, *matronly in* Iolanthe *and last night – determined to catch a man (and succeeding) was the perfect Lady Jane."*

"Christene Palmer, the Queen of the Fairies, finds, as its creator must have done, the touching characteristic in those contralto parts."
The Washington Post

Baked Tagliatelle

with Tomato and Aubergine Sauce

Ingredients

4 tbsp. oil

1 large onion, chopped

1¼ lb. Aubergines, diced (not peeled)

1½ LB. Tomatoes, peeled and chopped

1 fat clove of garlic, crushed

1½ tsp of dried basil

2 rounded tbsp. tomato puree

About 1 tbsp. sugar

2 oz. pitted black olives, chopped

1 lb. Tagliatelle

2 oz. butter

3 oz. grated Parmesan

2 small balls of Mozzarella, diced

Salt and black pepper

Serves: 4-6

Heat oven: 180°C, Gas Mark 4

Norman Wilfred Wright was with the Company from 1969-71. He subsequently sang with Scottish Opera, Glyndebourne and the English National Opera.

With every Good wish from Christeve, P.S. I haven't got a recipe for "Kangaroo Casserole"!!!

Method

Heat oil in a large pan and gently fry onions for 5 mins. Add aubergine and cook for a further 5 mins. Stir in the tomatoes, garlic, basil and tomato puree. Season with S&P and a little sugar. Cover the pan and simmer gently for about 20 mins. until the mixture has reduced to a sauce-like consistency.

Meanwhile cook the pasta, drain throughly and toss with the butter, the Mozzarella and some Parmesan. Season with S&P and spread in the bottom of a large baking dish (2½-3" deep).

Cover with the sauce and sprinkle with the remaining Parmesan.

Bake in the oven for 15 mins.

Richard Suart

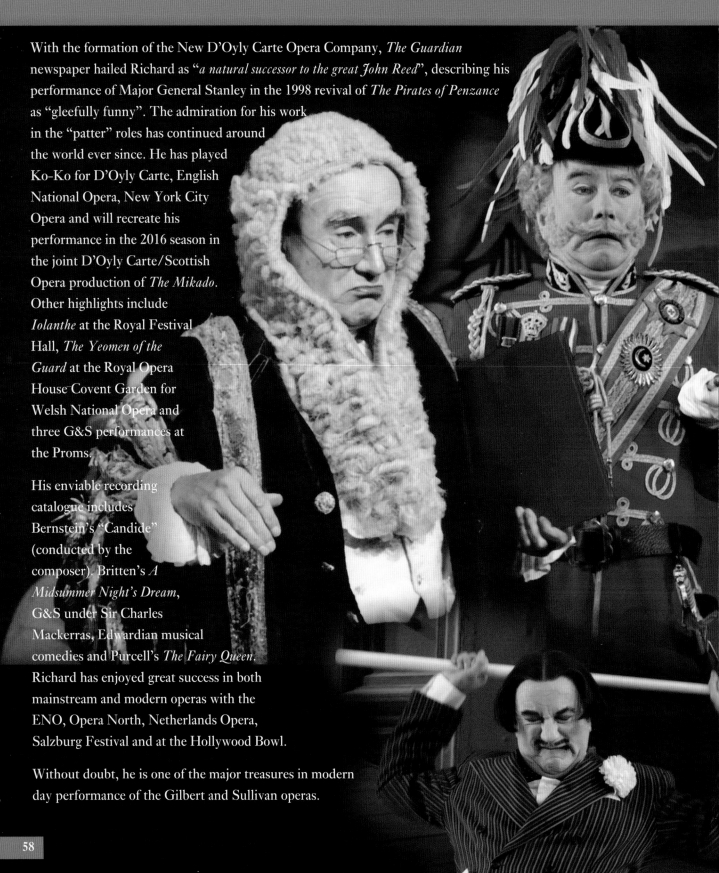

With the formation of the New D'Oyly Carte Opera Company, *The Guardian* newspaper hailed Richard as "*a natural successor to the great John Reed*", describing his performance of Major General Stanley in the 1998 revival of *The Pirates of Penzance* as "gleefully funny". The admiration for his work in the "patter" roles has continued around the world ever since. He has played Ko-Ko for D'Oyly Carte, English National Opera, New York City Opera and will recreate his performance in the 2016 season in the joint D'Oyly Carte/Scottish Opera production of *The Mikado*. Other highlights include *Iolanthe* at the Royal Festival Hall, *The Yeomen of the Guard* at the Royal Opera House Covent Garden for Welsh National Opera and three G&S performances at the Proms.

His enviable recording catalogue includes Bernstein's "Candide" (conducted by the composer), Britten's *A Midsummer Night's Dream*, G&S under Sir Charles Mackerras, Edwardian musical comedies and Purcell's *The Fairy Queen*. Richard has enjoyed great success in both mainstream and modern operas with the ENO, Opera North, Netherlands Opera, Salzburg Festival and at the Hollywood Bowl.

Without doubt, he is one of the major treasures in modern day performance of the Gilbert and Sullivan operas.

Chris's Farfalle

I would cook occasionally for my family, and this was my son's favourite – it gave an evening off to his mother and I offer it in memory of them both. It is colourful and very appealing to children whilst including lots of goodness!

Ingredients (Serves 4)

- 300g Farfalle Pasta
- 30g butter
- 2 shallots (or 1 onion), diced
- 2 cloves of garlic, finely sliced
- 1 red pepper, diced or cut into strips and halved
- 1 yellow pepper, diced or cut into strips and halved
- 50g green beans or sugar-snap peas
- 70g Italian Parma Ham cut into strips
- 200ml half fat crème fraiche
- 100g freshly grated parmesan cheese
- Freshly ground black pepper
- Fresh basil leaves to garnish or include in dish

Method

Cook the pasta according to instructions on the packet.
Meanwhile melt the butter in a large casserole dish and sweat the shallots gently for 3 minutes. Add the green beans, red and yellow pepper and cook for a further 4 minutes stirring occasionally.

Stir in the Parma Ham, crème fraiche, parmesan cheese and freshly ground black pepper to taste.

Drain the pasta and stir well into the rest of the ingredients.

Heat through and garnish with fresh basil. Serve immediately.

This dish is delicious with warm Ciabatta bread and a watercress salad.

Lyndsie Holland

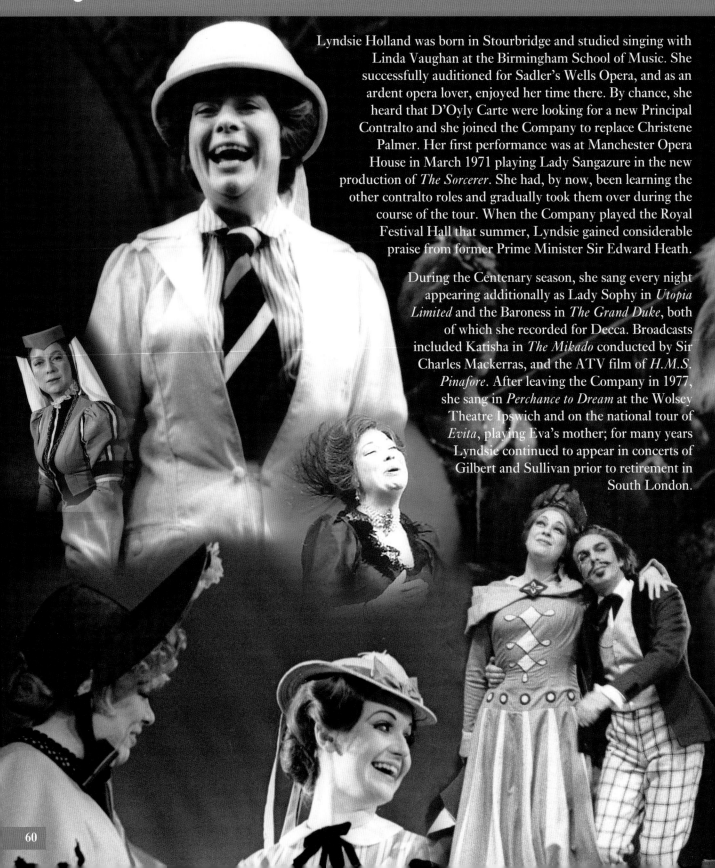

Lyndsie Holland was born in Stourbridge and studied singing with Linda Vaughan at the Birmingham School of Music. She successfully auditioned for Sadler's Wells Opera, and as an ardent opera lover, enjoyed her time there. By chance, she heard that D'Oyly Carte were looking for a new Principal Contralto and she joined the Company to replace Christene Palmer. Her first performance was at Manchester Opera House in March 1971 playing Lady Sangazure in the new production of *The Sorcerer*. She had, by now, been learning the other contralto roles and gradually took them over during the course of the tour. When the Company played the Royal Festival Hall that summer, Lyndsie gained considerable praise from former Prime Minister Sir Edward Heath.

During the Centenary season, she sang every night appearing additionally as Lady Sophy in *Utopia Limited* and the Baroness in *The Grand Duke*, both of which she recorded for Decca. Broadcasts included Katisha in *The Mikado* conducted by Sir Charles Mackerras, and the ATV film of *H.M.S. Pinafore*. After leaving the Company in 1977, she sang in *Perchance to Dream* at the Wolsey Theatre Ipswich and on the national tour of *Evita*, playing Eva's mother; for many years Lyndsie continued to appear in concerts of Gilbert and Sullivan prior to retirement in South London.

Duchess of Plaza–Toro

Ingredients

Large onion; 8 oz. lean beef mince; 1 carrot; 3 rashers of streaky bacon; standard sized tin of chopped tomatoes; tomato puree; 6 large mushrooms; sunflower oil; bay leaf; black pepper and mixed herbs. Pasta of your choice

Method

Finely chop the onion, cut the bacon rashers into small pieces and dice the mushrooms.

Heat just enough sunflower oil to cover the bottom of the saucepan and add the onion; stir continuously until soft but not brown.

Add the bacon and stir until sizzling. Season with black pepper.

Now add the mince and stir until it isn't red anymore! Still stirring, add the tinned tomatoes followed by the diced mushrooms. While simmering, cut the carrot into thin strips using a potato peeler and drop directly into the pan and stir.

Add two good squirts of tomato puree, throw in a bay leaf and a sprinkling of mixed herbs. When bubbling, turn down the heat for a 40 minute simmer and add a teaspoonful of white sugar.

Stir occasionally.

When cooked, leave to stand.

Cook the pasta in the usual way while keeping a colander in boiling hot water at the sink ready for draining.

"Serve, eat and enjoy!! Have any recording of Placido Domingo in the background."

Lyndsie (centre) with (L to R) Geoffrey Shovelton, Christene Palmer, John Ayldon, Gillian Knight, Thomas Round and Patricia Leonard

Love from
Lyndsie

David Mackie

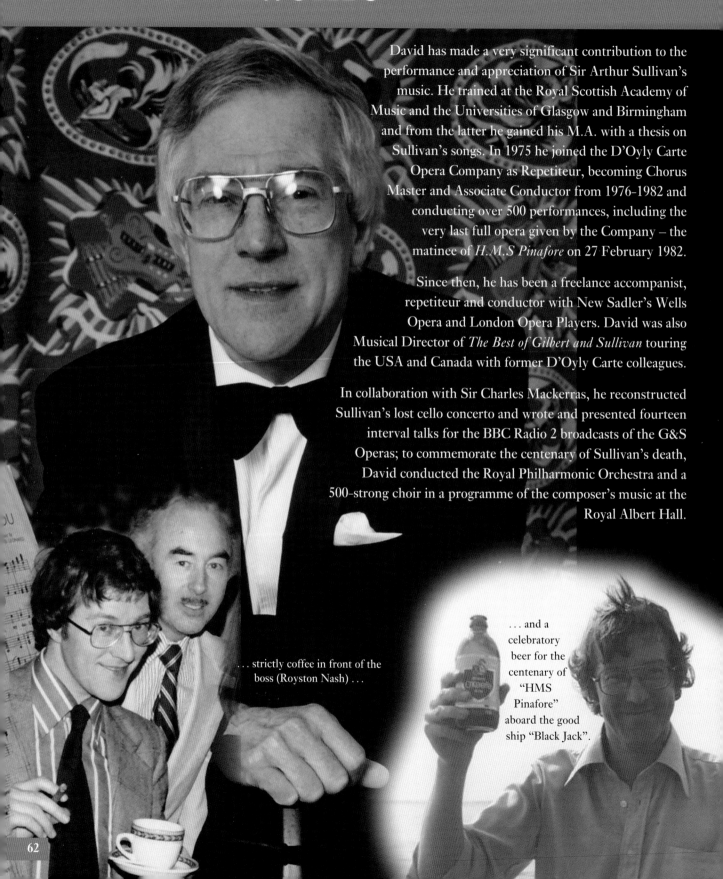

David has made a very significant contribution to the performance and appreciation of Sir Arthur Sullivan's music. He trained at the Royal Scottish Academy of Music and the Universities of Glasgow and Birmingham and from the latter he gained his M.A. with a thesis on Sullivan's songs. In 1975 he joined the D'Oyly Carte Opera Company as Repetiteur, becoming Chorus Master and Associate Conductor from 1976–1982 and conducting over 500 performances, including the very last full opera given by the Company – the matinee of *H.M.S Pinafore* on 27 February 1982.

Since then, he has been a freelance accompanist, repetiteur and conductor with New Sadler's Wells Opera and London Opera Players. David was also Musical Director of *The Best of Gilbert and Sullivan* touring the USA and Canada with former D'Oyly Carte colleagues.

In collaboration with Sir Charles Mackerras, he reconstructed Sullivan's lost cello concerto and wrote and presented fourteen interval talks for the BBC Radio 2 broadcasts of the G&S Operas; to commemorate the centenary of Sullivan's death, David conducted the Royal Philharmonic Orchestra and a 500-strong choir in a programme of the composer's music at the Royal Albert Hall.

. . . strictly coffee in front of the boss (Royston Nash) . . .

. . . and a celebratory beer for the centenary of "HMS Pinafore" aboard the good ship "Black Jack".

Spaghetti Palmieri

Spaghetti Palmieri

Ingredients

½ lb minced beef
2 medium sized mushrooms
1 medium sized onion
1 large tin of chopped tomatoes
Tomato purée
Sea salt
Black pepper

4 bay leaves
One teaspoon chopped basil
One teaspoon chopped oregano
½ teaspoon garlic granules
Parmesan cheese
Spaghetti
Vegetable oil

Preparation

Slice the onion and heat gently in the oil. Add the mince and turn until brown, then add the mushrooms, chopped tomatoes and tomato purée. Next add the bay leaves, basil, oregano and garlic, and season with salt and pepper. Simmer gently for about 30 minutes. After about 15 minutes prepare the spaghetti, allowing approximately 100 strands per person. Add to a pan of boiling water; this should take about 10-15 minutes. Drain the spaghetti, add the sauce (having first removed the bay leaves) and top off with parmesan cheese.

This quantity provides two portions. Buon appetito!

David Mackie

Meston Reid

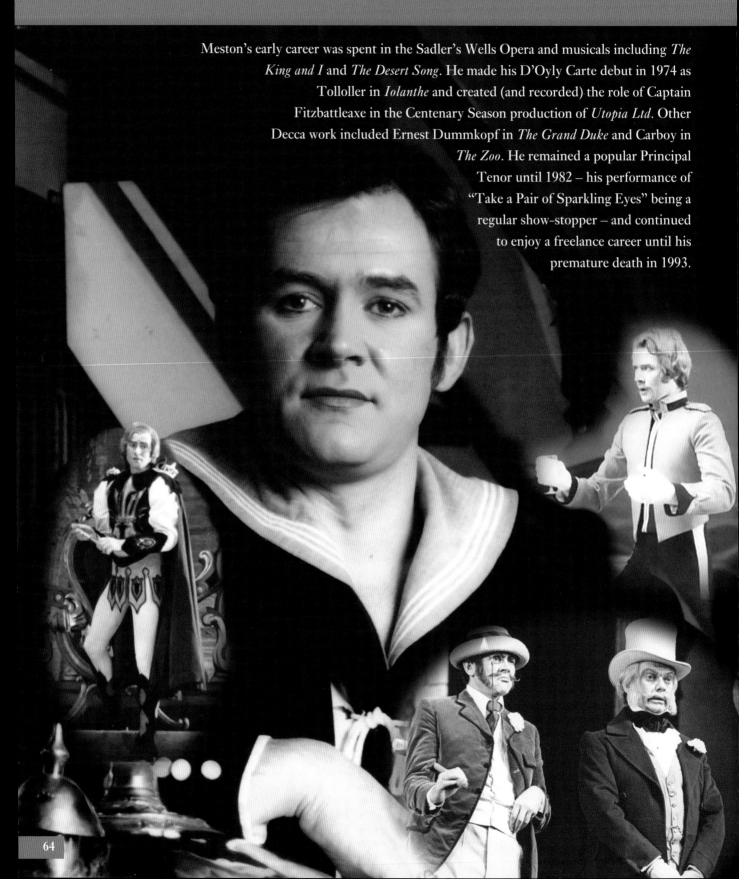

Meston's early career was spent in the Sadler's Wells Opera and musicals including *The King and I* and *The Desert Song*. He made his D'Oyly Carte debut in 1974 as Tolloller in *Iolanthe* and created (and recorded) the role of Captain Fitzbattleaxe in the Centenary Season production of *Utopia Ltd*. Other Decca work included Ernest Dummkopf in *The Grand Duke* and Carboy in *The Zoo*. He remained a popular Principal Tenor until 1982 – his performance of "Take a Pair of Sparkling Eyes" being a regular show-stopper – and continued to enjoy a freelance career until his premature death in 1993.

Meston's Boil and Bung

Spaghetti for Wandering Minstrels

Reed 'n' Reid

Ingredients

Tin of bolognaise sauce
"Quick" spaghetti

Method

Boil a kettle of water.
Empty the tin of ready-made sauce into a saucepan and heat gently.
Place the boiling water into another saucepan. Add the spaghetti.
When the water returns to the boil, turn down and simmer.
Test the spaghetti after the maker's recommended time.
Put the two together and devour.

"Ideal when on tour!"

John Owen Edwards

John was the popular and much respected Music Director of the D'Oyly Carte for 11 years during which time his extensive experience helped him raise to new heights the orchestral and vocal standard of the Company. Under his guidance, new productions by other European composers entered the repertoire, notably Offenbach's *Orpheus in the Underworld* and *La Vie Parisienne*, *Die Fledermaus* (Johann Strauss II) and *The Count of Luxembourg* (Franz Léhar). His many West End successes include *Annie*, *Chess*, *The Mitford Girls*, *Anything Goes*, *The Phantom of the Opera* and *The King and I* and he has recorded over 30 musicals, most notably *Kismet* with the Philharmonia, and *Oklahoma* for the National Theatre. In the world of opera, he has enjoyed a long and fruitful association with the Vienna Volksoper as Guest Conductor and Orchestrator as well as working with the Victoria State Opera, Opéra du Rhin and conducting an album of French arias with Valerie Masterson.

In every aspect of musical theatre, John's contribution has been immense; in the kitchen, however, he admits to a much more limited repertoire and unashamedly prefers dinner at the Ivy!

A Plate of Macaroni

and a Rusk

"When I first put this uniform on"

John with the DC Dining Club

Ingredients

480g flour
20ml baking powder
200g white sugar
Pinch of salt

35g aniseed
180g margarine
2 x large eggs
150ml milk

Method

1. Pre-heat the oven to 180C.
2. Sift the flour, baking powder and salt; mix in the sugar and aniseed then rub in the margarine with your fingertips.
3. Beat together the eggs and milk; mix all the ingredients together with a table knife until stiff.
4. Divide into long rolls approx 2cm in diameter and place on a baking tray.
5. Bake for 20 mins or until golden brown.
6. Allow to cool; divide into 1cm–wide slices then return them to a moderate temperature oven (150C) for 30 mins or until crisp.

For the macaroni: boil a saucepan of water (very lightly salted) and add the dry pasta. Cook for up to 10 mins. Season to taste and add a knob of butter. Add a sprinkling of Worcestershire sauce to finish. Serve with salad of choice.

John's alternative ...
"I think my ideal recipe is still 'Book a Table at the Ivy' - but this one is great!"

John Owen Edwards

'I don't want any lunch ...'
Pooh Bah: The Mikado

Leo Darnton

"Hush-a-bye Bacon"
Yours sincerely
Leo Darnton

M
E
A
T

Yorkshire Pudding & Gravy

69

Marjorie Eyre

Marjorie Eyre was born in Derby and joined the D'Oyly Carte in 1924 as a soprano chorister. In 1929 she re-trained as a mezzo-soprano and took over the roles with which she would be associated for the rest of her career – Iolanthe, Lady Angela, Cousin Hebe, Tessa, Mad Margaret et al. With her husband Leslie Rands she was part of the Company's glamorous dream-team, staying with the Carte for 22 years (both of them having turned down an offer to join MGM in 1934). They also toured together with the J.C. Williamson Company in Australia and New Zealand. Marjorie died in Brighton in 1987.

Baked Lamb Chops

loin lamb chops 1" thick
1 oz fat (½ oil ½ butter)
2 Onions
¾ lb canned tomatoes
½ tsp salt
¾ tsp pepper
1 tsp. sugar
2 ozs grated cheese
2 ozs fresh breadcrumbs

Trim off excess fat & remove bone (can be left on)

Peel & slice onions
Grate cheese & prepare breadcrumbs
Brown chops in hot fat & then place in large shallow casserole in single layer
Put several slices of onion on top of each chop - Pour on tomatoes add seasoning & sugar. Mix cheese & breadcrumbs & sprinkle over top - cover & bake slowly for 1½ hours in oven - Gas No 3 Elec. 300

Recipe for Melvyn

With love from,
Marjorie.

With Mary Godfrey
at *Sullivan's* –
Melvyn Tarran's restaurant

Vivian Tierney

Vivian made her professional debut with the D'Oyly Carte, and early performances as Lady Ella, Josephine, Mabel and Princess Ida made such a favourable impression that she was soon promoted to Principal Soprano and will always be remembered for her world-class rendition of "Poor Wand'ring One" – not least at the farewell performance at the Adelphi Theatre in 1982. She was much respected by her colleagues who thrived on her lively, vibrant portrayals and appreciated her outstanding acting ability. She would return in 1988 as a founder member of the New D'Oyly Carte Opera Company.

This was to be the start of an enviable international career; at home she enjoyed success with the English National Opera (especially as Tatiana in *Eugene Onegin* and Katerina in *Lady Macbeth of Mtsensk*), the Royal Opera, Glyndebourne and Scottish Opera and was a star of the New Sadler's Wells Opera. Across Europe, her notable successes include the Marschallin in *Der Rosenkavalier* and further performances of one of her signature roles - Ellen Orford in *Peter Grimes*, further enhancing her reputation in the operas of Benjamin Britten. She has sung across the USA and Canada including the title role in *The Gypsy Princess* (Opera Pacific), *Elektra* (Washington) and *The Turn of the Screw* in Santiago.

Lancashire Hotpot

Ingredients

100g dripping or butter

900g stewing lamb, cut into large chunks

3 lamb kidneys, sliced, fat removed (optional)

2 medium onions, chopped

4 carrots, peeled and sliced

25g plain flour

2 tsp Worcestershire sauce

500ml lamb or chicken stock

2 bay leaves

900g potatoes, peeled and sliced

Method

1. Heat oven to 160C/fan 140C/gas 3. Heat some dripping or butter in a large shallow casserole dish, brown the lamb in batches, lift to a plate, and then repeat with the kidneys.
2. Fry the onions and carrots in the pan with a little more dripping until golden. Sprinkle over the flour; allow cooking for a couple of mins, shaking over the Worcestershire sauce, pouring in the stock, and then bringing to the boil. Stir in the meat and bay leaves, and then turn off the heat. Arrange the sliced potatoes on top of the meat, and then drizzle with a little more dripping. Cover, then place in the oven for about 1½ hrs until the potatoes are cooked.
3. Remove the lid, brush the potatoes with a little more dripping, then turn the oven up to brown the potatoes, or finish under the grill for 5-8 mins until brown.

"Suzanne O'Keefe and I cooked Lancashire Hotpot in our London digs we were sharing, for the first time in 1975 when we were new choristers and rehearsing. We made it for a few colleagues including Paul Burrows, Kevin West, Glenis Prendergast and a couple more."

Neville and Elizabeth Griffths

Liz and Neville were married in 1953 when working together as members of the D'Oyly Carte. Neville had been made Principal Tenor in 1950 playing Nanki-Poo, Ralph Rackstraw, Frederic and Marco whilst Liz joined as a chorister but also played smaller roles such as Lady Saphir in *Patience*, Kate in *Pirates*, and, at one point, substituting for Ann Drummond-Grant as the Duchess of Plaza-Toro. Together, they left D'Oyly Carte in 1958 to join Sadler's Wells Opera staying for the move to the London Coliseum and the creation of the English National Opera, at times still performing Gilbert and Sullivan (*The Mikado*, *Iolanthe* and *Patience*). This much-loved couple retired to Liz's home town of Cheltenham and it was there that Neville died in 2010.

CAWL

900g Mutton (cubed)

900g Potatoes (cut into chunks)

2 Onions (chopped)

4 lg carrots (chopped)

1 Swede (chopped)

2 lg parsnips (chopped)

2 lg leeks (sliced)

½ bunch parsley (chopped)

Stock (use 3-4 cubes - veg) or lamb)

salt & pepper to taste

Bring mutton to boil in large pan with 5-6 pts water — skim

Add potatoes, onions, carrots, swede, parsnips & stock — simmer for 2-3 hours.

Add leeks & parsley & simmer for another 30 min

Add salt & pepper, you can also add a heaped teaspoon of curry powder if you wish.

Serve with warm crusty bread & lots of cheese

Enjoy.

God Bless,

Elizabeth & Neville

Neville's 'before and after' photo

Ralph Mason

Ralph Mason was born in Brighton and signed up for National Service in 1957 during which time he became a Corporal and served as Personal Secretary to Montgomery of Alamein.

His first encounter with Gilbert and Sullivan was at school where he played Ralph Rackstraw opposite Howard Blake, composer of *The Snowman*. From 1959–1961 he toured in the D'Oyly Carte Chorus prior to playing Freddie Eynsford-Hill in *My Fair Lady* at Drury Lane. He rejoined the D'Oyly Carte Opera Company as Principal Tenor in 1965 enjoying great success, particularly as Tolloller in *Iolanthe*, the Duke in *Patience* and Alexis in *The Sorcerer*. His final appearances were at the Savoy for the Centenary Season.

After a few years freelancing (including *The Privateer* for the BBC and *Coronation Street* for Granada), he joined the Welsh National Opera where he remained until retiring in 2003. In 2011 he published *Aspects of Life – Verse and Worse* and more recently his autobiography – *The Savoyard and the Sausage* or *I was Monty's Trouble*.

Sussex Bacon Pudding

Method

Prepare a suet pudding pastry (either vegetarian or ordinary) and roll out flat.

Cut the rind off the streaky bacon (smoked or unsmoked) and spread over the whole area of the suet.

Add plenty of sage & onion or parsley & thyme stuffing.

Steam in a muslin cloth until cooked.

Serve with carrots, parsnips and potatoes and a sweet white wine (Sauternes is best).

"It's a very cheap but filling meal and highly recommended. Ordinary back or shoulder will do or the packs of bacon off-cuts described as 'cooking bacon' available at all supermarkets."

Ralph Mason

On the town with Glyn Adams

Webster Booth

Webster Booth was born in Handsworth, Birmingham in 1902 and spent five years as a chorister at Lincoln Cathedral before studying singing at the Midland Institute. It was in Birmingham that he auditioned for the D'Oyly Carte and made his professional stage debut with them in September 1923. After four years of playing only minor roles he left the Company but did return to sing Luiz in the 1931 recording of *The Gondoliers*. His personal recording contract with HMV lasted until 1951 and included "Take a Pair of Sparkling Eyes" from the same opera.

His flourishing career embraced West End musical comedies including Rudolf Friml's *The Three Musketeers* and he made his film debut with Buster Keaton in *Invader*. On the concert platform he was a favourite of Sir Malcolm Sargent and with his wife Anne Ziegler, he enjoyed considerable popular success in the recording studio, operetta and film. Their tours took the "sweethearts in song" round the UK, Canada, Australia, New Zealand and South Africa, where they would eventually settle for over twenty years.

Returning to England in 1978, they were again in demand on television and radio and went on tour at the respective ages of 76 and 68! They made their home in Llandudno and were loyal supporters of our *Gilbert & Sullivan For All* concerts in that area, always occupying front row seats. Webster died in 1984, Anne lived on until 2003.

Brummie Cake

Ingredients

8oz (225 gms) Self-raising flour
3oz (85gms) Cheddar cheese
3oz (85 gms) Streaky bacon
1oz (28gms) Butter
5fl ozs (150ml) Milk
1 tbsp Tomato ketchup
¼ tsp Salt
Splash Worcester sauce
1 tbs Milk to coat

Method

Heat the oven to 200 degrees (Gas Mark 6) and grease a baking tray.
Grate the cheese, sift the flour and chop the butter into small pieces.
Fry the bacon until crispy and cut into small bits.
Put the flour into a mixing bowl and add the salt & butter; work with
the fingers until all blended together.
In a separate bowl, now mix the ketchup, milk and Worcester sauce.
Add this, the bacon and approx. one third of the cheese to the flour mix
and work well together until a nice dough is formed.
Using a floured surface or bread board, roll the dough in the flour then
roll out to a circular shape.
Brush with milk and put the remaining cheese over the top.
Place on the baking tray and place in the oven for half an hour.
Serve on its own or with eggs cooked your own favourite way.

Every Good Wish
Sincerely Yours
Webster Booth

Bruce Graham and

Madeleine Hudson

Bruce was born in Edinburgh and was a member of the D'Oyly Carte Opera Company from 1979–82; his work there included understudying Kenneth Sandford which gave him the opportunity to play, on occasion, some of the roles he would perfect later in his career – notably Pooh Bah and Don Alhambra. He also played Notary in *The Sorcerer* and Sergeant of Police in *The Pirates of Penzance* – now considered to be one of his signature roles.

He went on to enjoy success in the West End in *Me and My Girl*, *Follies* and *Cats* before returning to Gilbert and Sullivan with the Carl Rosa Opera. Now recognized as an experienced and valued exponent of the Savoy Operas, he is an invaluable member of the National Gilbert and Sullivan Opera Company and a favourite personality at the International G&S Festival.

Bruce and Madeleine (Caroline) met in the D'Oyly Carte, Madeleine having joined as a mezzo-soprano chorister in 1976. She occasionally appeared as Ada in *Princess Ida*, Kate in *Pirates*, Lady Saphir in *Patience* and Pitti-Sing in *The Mikado* prior to leaving in 1981.

Bruce and Caroline's Sausage Maryland

Ingredients (Serves 4)

8 Sausages of choice (we're very partial to a Cumberland link)

8 rashers streaky bacon (non-smoked)

4 bananas

100g plain flour

1 tsp baking powder

1 medium egg

150ml milk

200g can of sweetcorn (drained)

Butter or oil for frying

Kenneth Sandford gets tough with Brucie on the Last Night of the 1981 London Season

Method

Grill the sausages to a light to medium brown, set aside and keep warm. Grill the non-smoked streaky bacon until the fat clarifies, but remove from the grill before the fat goes brown. Wrap a rasher round each sausage and finish off under the grill until the bacon cooks thoroughly, turning as necessary. Set aside and keep warm. To prepare the sweetcorn fritters: Sift the flour, baking powder and seasoning into a large bowl. Make a well in the centre, add a medium egg and gradually beat in 150ml milk to form a smooth batter. Drain a 200g can of sweetcorn kernels, pat dry on a kitchen towel and add to the batter. Fry tablespoonfuls of the mixture in hot butter or oil for about 2 minutes each side until crisp and golden. Set aside and keep warm.

Slice the bananas lengthwise, coat in flour and fry until golden brown. Serve all the ingredients together with vegetables of choice, if required.

... displaying a well-turned calf during a confrontation between Dame Carruthers (Patricia Leonard) and Phoebe Meryll (Lorraine Daniels) in *The Yeomen of the Guard*.

Bon Apetit!

With all good wishes

Madeleine Hudson

Very best wishes

Bruce Graham

Bruce *"created this recipe for Caroline (who's stage name was then Madeleine Hudson) several times; romance blossomed to the sound of sizzling sausages and we have now been married for 30 years ..."*

John Ayldon

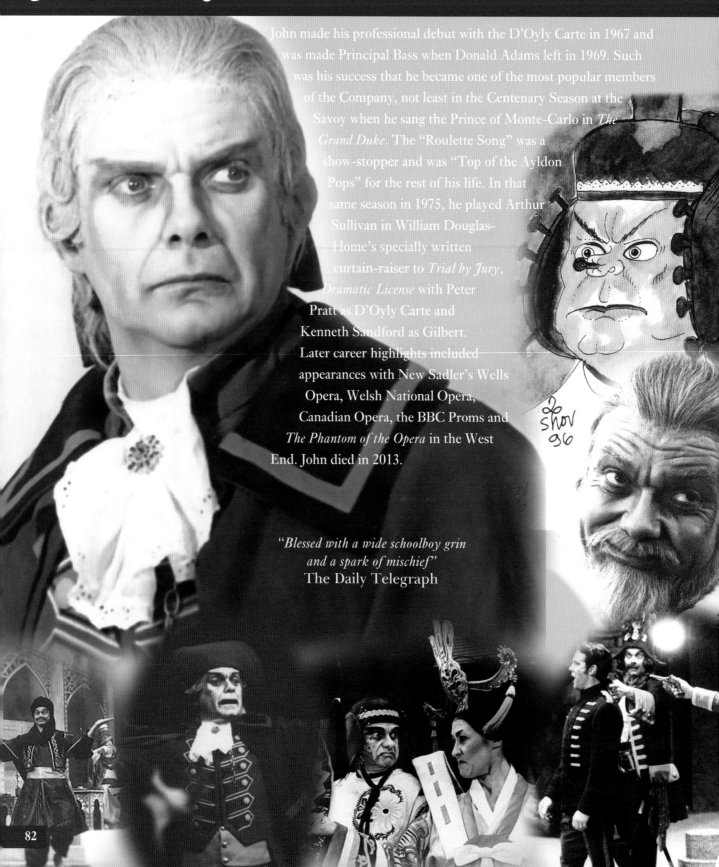

John made his professional debut with the D'Oyly Carte in 1967 and was made Principal Bass when Donald Adams left in 1969. Such was his success that he became one of the most popular members of the Company, not least in the Centenary Season at the Savoy when he sang the Prince of Monte-Carlo in *The Grand Duke*. The "Roulette Song" was a show-stopper and was "Top of the Ayldon Pops" for the rest of his life. In that same season in 1975, he played Arthur Sullivan in William Douglas-Home's specially written curtain-raiser to *Trial by Jury*, *Dramatic License* with Peter Pratt as D'Oyly Carte and Kenneth Sandford as Gilbert. Later career highlights included appearances with New Sadler's Wells Opera, Welsh National Opera, Canadian Opera, the BBC Proms and *The Phantom of the Opera* in the West End. John died in 2013.

"Blessed with a wide schoolboy grin and a spark of mischief"
The Daily Telegraph

Pork with Mushrooms

in a Sour Cream Brandy Sauce

"Let all your doubts take wing" –
rehearsing *Utopia Ltd*

FAVOURITE RECIPE:—
PORK WITH MUSHROOMS, ONIONS IN SOUR CREAM BRANDY SAUCE
INGREDIENTS   1 LB. BEST PORK FILLET.
 2 MEDIUM ONIONS.
 12oz BUTTON MUSHROOMS
 10oz CARTON SOUR CREAM
 BRANDY.   BUTTER FOR SAUTÉ. SEASONING.
METHOD SLICE PORK, ONIONS & MUSHROOMS. IN LARGE FRYPAN
MELT 2oz BUTTER & QUICKLY SAUTÉ PORK SLICES TO SEAL
ADD SLICED MUSHROOMS & CONTINUE SAUTÉ UNTIL BOTH COOKED
THOROUGHLY — ADD ONION RINGS & COOK OVER LOW HEAT
FURTHER 3-4 MINUTES. STRAIN OFF BUTTER. ADD SOUR
CREAM & REHEAT SLOWLY TILL BUBBLING. ADD BRANDY
& LIGHT SEASONING. SERVE 3-4 WITH POTATO & VEG.

This dish was served to me by my
dear landlady in Sunderland (a gourmet
cook!) I first stayed with her & her husband
in 1967 (with John Webley) & returned there
every time the D'Oyly Carte & Sadler's Wells
Opera visited Sunderland, Billingham &
occasionally Newcastle.

John Ayldon

John launching into his
party-piece . . . the
Roulette Song from
The Grand Duke

Abby Hadfield

Abby is from Macclesfield, trained at the Royal Manchester College of Music (now the Royal Northern) and joined the D'Oyly Carte in 1963, initially as a chorister. She then understudied Peggy Ann Jones and Pauline Wales as Hebe, Edith, Pitti–Sing, Lady Angela and Tessa. In time, she played Ada in *Princess Ida*, Vittoria in *The Gondoliers* and Isabel in *The Pirates of Penzance* and was with the Company for the innovative season at the Royal Festival Hall in 1971. To this day, she remains a much-loved personality amongst her former G&S colleagues and has enjoyed a varied career in all aspects of musical theatre, drama and entertainment.

Pork Carbonade Javanaise

and Kyrenian Meat Dish

Pork Carbonade Javanaise: Ingredients, Serves 4 (halve the recipe for two).

Can of celery or fresh (about two hearts, sliced) the latter makes the dish more crunchy.

2 medium onions, chopped

2 oz butter, Juice of ¼ lemon

Teaspoon of curry powder (or to your taste) – the dish is only supposed to have a hint of curry – very mild.

1 soupspoon of flour

Curl of orange peel, finely sliced into strips

Cup of stock (I use chicken or pork – nothing too strong)

½ cup of milk, 2 tablespoons of cream

4 pork steaks (cut from the leg)

Method

Brown the pork steaks in butter, salt them and put on one side in a casserole.

Mix the flour and curry powder.

Fry the onions and celery together with the orange peel in the same pan used for the pork steaks. When golden and getting soft, mix in the flour and curry powder, slowly stir in the stock and finally add the milk. Pour the mixture over the steaks, cover and leave to gently simmer, do not let it dry out. Cook for not less then 30 mins or more than 45 mins until the steaks are tender.

Just before serving, stir in the cream and lemon juice. Serve with fluffy rice.

Kyrenian Meat Dish: Ingredients, Serves 4

1 lb lean minced beef or lamb

4 Large tomatoes, skinned, de-seeded, and chopped

1 Large grated onion, 1 Large finely chopped green pepper

1 teaspoon nutmeg (alter to taste), 1 pinch of garlic salt or 1 crushed clove of garlic (not too much, otherwise the fragrance of the nutmeg is lost), 1 Large bay leaf crushed,

7 crushed peppercorns, 1 pinch mixed herbs

2 Tablespoons of tomato puree

½ glass of red wine

2 Tablespoons of plain flour, 1 chicken stock cube

6 ozs cheddar cheese

Salt, Cooking oil

Abby Hadjield

Method

Gently heat a little cooking oil in a large saucepan.

Fry the tomatoes, onion and green pepper slowly – soften don't brown, add herbs, bay leaf, peppercorns, nutmeg and tomato purée. Stir and then add the red wine. Add the meat and cook slowly for 15 minutes.

Mix the flour into a thin paste with cold water and add this to the mixture. Then add a cupful of warm water together with the crushed stock cube. Cook gently for another 5 minutes.

Transfer the entire mixture to an earthenware dish (off the heat) and grate half the cheese over the mixture and allow to sink in for about 15 minutes – do not stir! Grate the rest of the cheese (more if you want to) and place the dish in the oven at 325F and cook for about 40 minutes. I usually cover the meal at this point so it doesn't burn or dry out.

Finally, take off the cover, turn up the oven to 400F to brown the cheese.

Serve with rice.

It will freeze but add cheese on the top when reheating and brown under the grill.

"I love this dish because of the different flavouring you get from the nutmeg. It leaves a luxuriant smell in the kitchen and titillates your guests' taste buds should you serve this for a dinner party."

David Steadman

David first conducted G&S with John Reed and the D'Oyly Carte Principals and *Gilbert and Sullivan For All* with Donald Adams and Thomas Round. He co-produced the memorable reunion concert *Together Again* at Manchester Free Trade Hall prior to joining the New D'Oyly Carte Opera Company in 1994. Since then, he has served the D'Oyly Carte Trust as Chorus Master, Principal Conductor and Production Musical Director at the Savoy, Sadler's Wells, Royal Festival Hall and on tour, as well as the joint productions with Scottish Opera.

In the West End, USA, Australia and around Europe, he has conducted many musicals including *Wonderful Town*, *Evita*, *A Little Night Music*, *Love Never Dies* and *The Sound of Music*, enjoying a wonderful 35-year association with his mentor, producer Bill Kenwright.

David always found time to return to G&S, especially in concerts with Patricia Leonard, John Ayldon & Ken Sandford, and has conducted at many of the International Gilbert & Sullivan Festivals.

Seated at the piano once owned by Fanny Ronalds, Sir Arthur Sullivan's long-term friend and lover. The piano is a major feature of the Melvyn Tarran Collection.

Black Pudding with Potatoes

Served with a Guinness and Onion Gravy

Ingredients

Gravy

Medium size onion
125ml Draught Guinness
250ml Beef Stock
3 x tbs Plain Flour
3 x tbs Butter

Potatoes and Black Pudding

900g large potatoes
Large onion, sliced thinly and halved
4 x thick slices of black pudding
4 x slices of mature cheddar cheese
6 x tbs vegetable oil
3 x tbs butter
Salt & pepper to taste

Method

1. Gravy: Melt the butter in a saucepan, add the onions but don't let them brown. Add the flour and stir until the flour disappears. Now add the Guinness and the stock; boil then reduce to a medium heat. Stir constantly until thick; keep warm on a very low heat, stirring occasionally.
2. Potatoes and Black Pudding: part-boil the potatoes for five minutes. Gently heat the oil and butter in a frying pan; rinse the potatoes under the cold tap, allow to cool then grate into coarse pieces and mix with the onion.
3. Grill the black pudding on both sides and top with the cheese; cover each slice (all over) with some of the potato mix and fry in the fat until both sides are brown.

Paying off college fees in
The Student Prince with Pamela Field.

" actin' " with Miss Leonard!

With "adopted aunt", Ella Halman

Stourbridge duo . . . David and
Lyndsie Holland – fashion icons!!

Philip Potter

After singing in the West End productions of *Where's Charley?*, *Marigold*, *Flower Drum Song* and *Chu Chin Chow*, Philip joined D'Oyly Carte as Principal Tenor in 1961. His good looks, silky voice and stage charisma made him an instant hit with audiences and he was a great favourite of Bridget D'Oyly Carte. He broadcast regularly on the Welsh television programme *A Land of Song*, sang the Duke in the BBC 2 screening of *Patience* from the Saville Theatre and was Nanki-Poo in the Company's film of *The Mikado*. He recorded several of his roles for Decca enjoying particular success opposite Valerie Masterson in the 1968 *The Pirates of Penzance*. After leaving the Company in 1970, he returned several times as Guest Artist, especially for the Centenary Season at the Savoy and the 1979 tour of Australia and New Zealand.

Jugged Hare

Jugged Hare (Civet de lièvre)

To prepare marinade: Brandy, wine or port, sliced onions and garlic. celery sticks, 4 bay leaves, bouquet garni salt and peppercorns and some hare blood

Cut the hare into sections and immerse in the marinade for 24 hours.

Fry some diced lean bacon and onions until light brown; dry the hare pieces and gently sauté sprinkle with flour add some red wine and red currant jelly

Place hare and bacon etc into a heavy earthenware casserole dish add remainder of blood, black pepper, rind of lemon, mace and cover with water. Cover casserole with tight fitting lid and cook at gas mark 3 or 335° for 2 to 3 hours until hare is tender

For the liason: 2 oz butter, 2 oz flour, ¼ port wine, 1 tablespoon red currant jelly; work the butter and flour into a smooth paste — add the strained juices from the casserole

Serve with croutons, veg etc. Philip Potter

Ella Halman and Radley Flynn

Ella studied at the Brighton School of Music on a scholarship prior to joining the Carl Rosa Opera Company. After further training at the Royal College of Music she successfully auditioned for D'Oyly Carte in 1937 and took over the role of Inez from Josephine Curtis. In an emergency, she was asked to go on as the Duchess in *The Gondoliers* which she prepared in one afternoon and played the same evening. She was then made understudy to Evelyn Gardiner and became Principal Contralto when the Company reconvened after the outbreak of the Second World War. Her first few seasons were fraught with danger – "*during air raids, the audience was given the opportunity to leave, but we had to carry on! In Exeter, our digs were flattened the morning we left, and in Hull, we were trapped in the theatre one night until 1a.m. When we were allowed to leave, there wasn't a window left in the street – we trudged home in the dark almost knee-deep in glass.*" Despite these conditions, she gained great popularity with audiences and colleagues; after recording all her roles for Decca, she bowed out at the end of the Festival of Britain season at the Savoy and went to America with Martyn Green, to appear in S.M. Chartock's Productions of *Iolanthe*, *The Mikado*, *The Pirates of Penzance* and *H.M.S. Pinafore*. She later returned to England and lived happily in Cumbria until her death in 1995. Ella Halman was a contralto in the true English tradition.

"*Her voice was like a great bell swinging in a dome*"
"*Ella Halman well-earned the warm recognition extended to her*"

"*I, for one, lost my heart to Ella Halman*"
USA Press Reviews

Radley Flynn was born in Rochdale in 1902 and was with the D'Oyly Carte Opera Company for 23 years from 1928-1951. He played many of the smaller roles including Old Adam, Go-To, Scynthius and Giorgio, tho' on numerous occasions he stood in for Sydney Granville, Darrell Fancourt, Richard Walker and Richard Watson. His was a resonant bass voice capable of "*rattling the floor boards*" according to Company member Frederick Sinden! In 1940, he married Ella Halman and, when they both left D'Oyly Carte, appeared with Martyn Green in the S.M. Chartock G&S productions in the USA. On their return, they moved up to Penrith where the air was fresh and the fishing was good – Radley died on his boat in 1978.

Cornish Pasty

with Chutney

Cornish Pasties.

4 oz good steak.
Small piece kidney
Small onion
1 medium potato
Half a carrot.

Grate carrot & potato, mince meat
and onion, mix together with salt
and pepper.
About 8 ozs. rough puff pastry.
Roll thin. Cut out circles with a
breakfast cup. Put small lump of
filling on each & seal the edges
tightly.
Make two small cuts in each
pasty, bake on a baking sheet for
about 20 minutes at 425°.

Chutney

3 lbs Cooking Apples
1 lb. Onions
½ lb raisins
½ " dates
1 oz salt
1 teaspoon ginger.
Tabasco sauce
Black pepper.
1 pt vinegar - spiced.
1 lb sugar.

Chop fruit & simmer with
seasonings in the vinegar until
soft & pulpy - about 1 hr.

*Best wishes Yours
Sincerely
Ella Flesmore*

Radley Flynn

These recipes, dictated by Ella and Radley, were
kindly supplied by Sheila Stanley, Radley's daughter,
pictured above as a toddler with her father.

Valerie Masterson C.B.E.

After training at the Royal College of Music and in Milan, Valerie spent a season with the Landestheatre Opera Company in Salzburg and sang at the Proms under Sir Malcolm Sargent. She was Principal Soprano with the D'Oyly Carte from 1964–69 melting and breaking hearts wherever she went! She was perfect in the roles she played – Yum-Yum, Mabel and Princess Ida rapidly becoming signature portrayals yet to be equalled. After leaving the Company she often returned as Guest Artist in *Princess Ida* and as Mabel in the 1981/2 season at the Adelphi Theatre. By this time, her operatic career was in full bloom at Glyndebourne, ENO, Opera North, Welsh National Opera, Royal Opera and in Paris, Toulouse, Milan, San Francisco etc. embracing the operas of Mozart, Handel, Verdi, Puccini, Massenet and Donizetti. Her impressive catalogue of recordings also extended to the classics of musical theatre. She was made a C.B.E. in 1988.

"She's adorable, she's pretty, she's utterly charming, she's a beautiful singer – she's Valerie Masterson!"
The Savoyard

"The mystique of Gilbert and Sullivan had always escaped me until I saw the D'Oyly Carte, but no more. Valerie Masterson's singing alone would have been enough to captivate me . . ."
Press Review; Washington DC

92

Barbecued Spare Ribs

Ingredients

3 to 4 lb. Spare ribs cut in serving pieces

1 lemon, sliced

1 large onion, sliced

1 cup tomato sauce [catsup]

3 tbsp. Worcestershire sauce

1 tsp. Chili powder

1 tsp. Salt

2 dashes of Tabasco

1 cup of water

Valerie with Peggy Ann Jones at the Buxton International G&S Festival.

Method

Heat oven to 450F [hot]. Place ribs in baking pan, meaty side up. On each piece, place a slice of lemon and onion. Roast 30 mins. Combine remaining ingredients; pour over the ribs. Reduce heat to 350 [mod] and bake 1hr. 30 mins more. Baste 2 or 3 times while baking.

Serves 4.

Valerie (right) with Christene Palmer and John Reed

"I have sent you one of my treasured recipes which I found in America on my first tour with D'Oyly Carte. It was there that I sampled for the first time the delicious hot sauce for prawn cocktails and having a passion for cookery books, I found a copy of a Betty Crocker cook book called Good and Easy.

Since then, every summer we have a family barbecue and they all insist on my spare ribs which I can honestly boast are the best in the world!"

With love

Valerie Mastersen

Pauline Wales

Within months of joining the D'Oyly Carte Chorus in 1959, Pauline played her first role in the operas – Isabel in *The Pirates of Penzance*. Soon after, she began to appear in roles with which she would be associated for much of her time with the Company – Leila, Cousin Hebe, Lady Saphir and Melissa in *Princess Ida*. From 1965, she became a popular Tessa in *The Gondoliers* notably in the new Antony Besch production three years later. Having left the D'Oyly Carte in 1974, she returned as a Guest Artiste in *Princess Ida* for the Centenary Season at the Savoy. She also performed with *Gilbert and Sullivan For All*, Kent Opera (Mad Margaret in *Ruddigore*) and was a most welcome guest at the 1993 Reunion Concert *Together Again* in Manchester.

Fire Alarm Chilli

FIRE ALARM CHILLI. (4-6)

4 fluid ozs Veg. Oil
2 lbs good braising steak - cubed
2 ozs Hot Chilli powder + 1oz flour
2 tspns ground Cumin
2 tspns dried Oregano
3 large Cloves Garlic crushed with Sea Salt
1 pint of beef stock
1 large can of chopped tomatoes
Freshly ground black pepper
6-8 green chillies + 1ge can
of red Kidney beans.

Heat oil in heavy based frying pan + brown meat in batches, very well - you may need more oil - transferring it into a heavy based casserole with a tight lid. Stir in the flour, chilli + Cumin seasoning, turning well over until very well coated. Add the Oregano, garlic, salt + green chillies, Stir well again, then add tomatoes and stock, and bring to the boil, cover, and simmer - very slowly for at least 2½-3 hrs - longer if possible. Add beans for about 30 mins before serving. I also add crème fraiche just before serving, and of course, very occasionally 4-6 small squares of dark chocolate. If a more "tomatoey" flavour is wanted - add some tomato puree.

"I'm including my Chilli recipe – everyone has one don't they?

It's fairly hot and tasty – I never use mince but good braising steak which I chop, or rather slice into 1 inch cubes! The recipe is, I think, Texan, where they serve the beans on the side and not mixed in."

Pauline Daniels.

Geoffrey Shovelton

After a career embracing oratorio, Scottish Opera, Chelsea Opera Group and appearances with *Gilbert & Sullivan For All*, Geoffrey joined D'Oyly Carte in 1975. So successful was he as Colonel Fairfax in *The Yeomen of the Guard* that it prompted the Carte management to press ahead with a new recording of the opera in 1979. His natural skills as a raconteur, familiar to many concert-goers, were put to excellent use on the 1978 recording of *The Zoo* whilst, for the last night of the 1982 season at the Adelphi, he had also designed and illustrated the farewell programme. His artistic talents have provided his many admirers with an array of witty Christmas cards for several years and numerous amateur companies have gained much from him as a Director and Producer. Geoffrey now lives in America with his wife Deborah.

Meat & Potato Pie

Certain dishes are powerfully evocative of my Lancashire childhood.

Mother made black-treacle toffee, to be sucked whilst watching the Guy Fawkes bonfire and fireworks. She swore by it, "for protecting the chest" (with occasional help from Stothert's "Lung Healers").

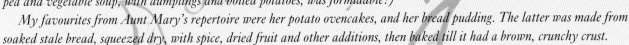

Aunt Agnes' family lived just around the corner, and her speciality was individual meat and potato pies, made fresh for eating when we got back from Christmas Midnight Mass.

But the cooking I tasted most often, outside home, was Aunt Mary's. She and another unmarried sister of my mother lived next door with my Granny Cullen (who had raised nine surviving children and was no slouch in the kitchen herself: her thick pea and vegetable soup, with dumplings and boiled potatoes, was formidable!)

My favourites from Aunt Mary's repertoire were her potato ovencakes, and her bread pudding. The latter was made from soaked stale bread, squeezed dry, with spice, dried fruit and other additions, then baked till it had a brown, crunchy crust.

In our house one of the most popular dishes, which therefore we had often, was the traditional Meat and Potato Pie of Lancashire. "Thus it ran".

Ingredients; (for 4 persons)

1lb shoulder steak potatoes as required ('floury' better than 'waxy')
1 large or 2 medium onions
salt, pepper (traditionally, white pepper)

Pastry as required, (Suet Crust or shortcrust: 6 to 8oz flour, 3 to 4oz fat, according to size of dish.)
stock, or water

Method

Cut the meat up into half-inch pieces, chop the onion, and put both into a deep pie dish. (The traditional pie dish used in Lancashire is the tall, brown on the outside, straight-sided one with the top's diameter slightly larger than that of the base.)

Peel the potatoes, but do not slice. Insert the blade, as if for slicing, but "crack off" fairly small pieces. (The resulting rough edge of the potato helps the pie juices to thicken better.)

Season with salt and pepper, mix well, and fill up to the top of the potato mixture with stock or water. Cover with a lid and cook in a moderate oven for two and a half hours.

Turn up the heat for the pie crust . Make a half-inch thick crust. Before putting this on the dish, give the meat and potato mixture a good stir. Return the pie to the oven to bake for 20 to 30 minutes, until the crust is done.

"My memory has been assisted, in providing this recipe, by a little book I bought in Lancaster Priory Church on 26 March 1979 – or so the flyleaf tells me. The title is Lancashire Cookery, published by Dalesman Books (1978), and complied by "Readers of The Dalesman". I have adapted it a little in order to produce the dish I remember.

When still a small boy, I read such comics as Dandy and Beano; "Desperate Dan" could always make me chuckle. I thought of him whenever we had Meat and Potato Pie because his mother made it with horns of the cow sticking out though the crust; mine could never be persuaded to garnish ours in quite the same way!"

Martyn Green

Martyn Green was a Londoner born in 1899 and served in the army during the Great War. After his stage debut in *The Rebel Maid*, he studied at the Royal College of Music and made his first West End appearance in revue at the London Palladium.

In 1922 he joined the D'Oyly Carte "New" Opera Company as a chorister and understudy before transferring to the main repertory company where he understudied Sir Henry Lytton. After Lytton's car accident in 1931, he was given the roles of Major General Stanley and Robin Oakapple, also playing many performances as Jack Point. He took over as Principal Comedian on Lytton's retirement until the outbreak of war in 1939, also appearing in Victor Schertzinger's film of *The Mikado*. With the temporary closure of provincial theatres, Rupert D'Oyly Carte cancelled the 1939 autumn tour and Martyn joined the cast of *Lights Up* for C.B. Cochran at the Savoy. After serving in the Royal Air Force he rejoined the D'Oyly Carte in 1946, staying until the end of the Festival of Britain Season in 1951. He appeared as Grossmith in the film *The Story of Gilbert & Sullivan* before moving to America to tour with Ella Halman and Radley Flynn in four operas for S.M. Chartock. He stayed in the US and lived in New York City for many years, moving to Hollywood in 1973.

He enjoyed a successful career on Broadway, television and film including *Red Peppers* with Ginger Rogers (directed by Otto Preminger), *Black Comedy*, *Canterbury Tales*, *Charley's Aunt*, and the 1973 movie *The Iceman Cometh*. He also directed Groucho Marx in *The Mikado* and made several more recordings including an album of children's songs with Julie Andrews. In 1959, his left leg was amputated below the knee after a lift accident at a garage where he was parking his MG. His final stage appearance was in Chicago in *The Sea* and he died in Hollywood on 8 February 1975.

He was famously acknowledged for his crystal clear diction and light-footed dancing (despite a leg injury during World War One) and his colleague, Ella Halman, was one of many to benefit from his brilliant timing.

Rehearsing in America with Ella Halman and Robert Rounseville

Steak and Kidney Pie

Ingredients (for a quick and simple recipe)

with mushrooms

1kg (2lbs) stewing steak;   800ml (27 fl oz) beef stock;

250g (8 oz) kidneys   250g (8 oz) mushrooms;

2 chopped onions;   250g (8 oz) smoked meat;

5 tbsp flour;   4 tbsp vegetable oil;

Pastry; salt; pepper; Bouquet Garni (or a Bay Leaf)

New York

Method

(if the mixture is prepared a day in advance, any excess fat can be removed before adding the pastry)

Peel off the outer membrane of the kidneys and clean out the inner white parts; chop up the rest.

Heat up the oil, add the smoked meat and onions until brown.

Rub the beef with 4 tbsp of flour and add to the pan until brown.

Dip the kidneys into the remaining flour; add to the pan until lightly browned.

Now add the beef stock and place the whole mixture into a casserole dish.

Add the Bouquet Garni/Bay Leaf and cook for 2 hrs at 160 degrees C.

Then remove from oven, extract the Bouquet Garni/Bay Leaf, add the mushrooms and leave for half an hour.

Line the rim of a pie dish with pastry; add the mixture (as much as required) and place your prepared pastry lid over the top. Make some ventilation holes with a fork.

Bake for 20 mins at 220 degrees C. Reduce the heat to 160 degrees C and cook for a further 15 mins.

Truth without Trimmings

⊞ ⊞ ⊞

Mr Martyn Green

of the

D'Oyly Carte Opera Company

What is your favourite theatre?
Savoy Theatre.

Which is your favourite play?
Scarlet Pimpernel.

What is your earliest recollection?
Sitting up in my pram.

Which is your favourite sport?
Riding and golf.

Which is your favourite hobby?
Reading thrillers.

Which are your favourite cigarettes?
Players—please!

What would you do to make Edinburgh brighter?
Can it be?

What is your ideal holiday?
Nothing to do and lots of time to do it.

Which is your lucky day?
Pay day!

Which is your favourite dish?
Steak and kidney pie—with mushrooms.

What is your greatest ambition?
To own at least one horse.

What is your favourite motto?
There is humour in all things—find it and make the most of it.

When do you feel at your worst?
Before a cold bath.

When do you feel at your best?
After a cold bath.

What is your favourite pet?
My wife.

What is your pet aversion?
Talking shop.

What is your opinion of bridge?
H——! (Deleted by Censor).

What, if you were not connected with the theatre, would you prefer to be?
Independent.

Which is your favourite Christian name?
Joy.

James Conroy Ward

James was the last patter man to serve the D'Oyly Carte Opera Company before the temporary closure in 1982. He was born in Timperley, Cheshire and both his father and grandfather had been on the stage; the latter was a music-hall comedian and appeared with George Grossmith. He made his D'Oyly Carte debut as a twelve year old at Manchester Opera House as the Midshipman in *H.M.S Pinafore* and as Ko-Ko's assistant in *The Mikado*. His first wage packet was for 10/6d and it didn't improve much when he joined the Company full-time in 1973! This came after training at the Royal Northern College of Music, winning the Imperial League of Opera Prize, further study at the London Opera Centre and four years with the Royal Opera, Covent Garden. He understudied John Reed and appeared as the Major General, Major Murgatroyd, Foreman of the Jury and Antonio until inheriting the patter roles after the Australian tour in 1979 – a position he felt privileged to hold.

Ward's Winter Warmer

INGREDIENTS :- ___700 — 800 grams SHIN BEEF + BONES___

4 Carrots
2 Large onions
1 Fennel bulb (optional)
1 Celery heart
Greek basil (optional)
Parsley
½ tsp. Mediterranean / Provencal herbs.
Black Pepper
Beef or vegetable stock
½ bottle red wine (optional
1½ tbps. Barley

> STEAM IN THE MICROWAVE for 6 minutes

Method.

1. Scrape the carrots, cut in chunks;
   Peel and slice onions; chop
   celery; chop fennel.
   Steam in the microwave or on the hob
   to "gently" soften.

2. Chop the meat and remove
   large pieces of fat or sinew.
   Keep 1 or 2 rings of marrow bone shin.

3. Put the meat in the casserole plus
   herbs, chopped parsley, basil and
   black pepper adding the drained
   vegetables.

4. Cover with stock (and wine if using;

5. Add the barley and stir together with
   bones.

6. Cover with foil lightly + lid
   or 2 layers of foil.

7. Place in the oven.
   Gas 1. Electric. 100. for 4·5 hours.
   Check & stir.

8. Taste for seasoning, add salt.

Serve with :- Crusty Bread, boiled
   or Jacket potatoes.

Add. 1 tin of drained butter
beans if desired.
Chop parsley and scatter on top.!

This will reheat in the microwave
& freeze well. Defrost Thoroughly
before cooking.

Enjoy

James Renory - Ward

101

Pamela Field

After studying at the Welsh College of Music and Drama and the Royal College of Music (also winning the Young Welsh Singers Competition and the Pernod Award), Pamela joined the D'Oyly Carte in 1972 as an understudy, becoming Principal Soprano a year later. Her regular roles were Josephine, Patience, Phyllis, Elsie Maynard and Gianetta but she was lucky enough to play Princess Zara in *Utopia Ltd* and the Princess of Monte Carlo in *The Grand Duke* for the Centenary Season at the Savoy. Her clear and pure vocal tone was much enjoyed by audiences; after leaving the Company, Pamela had a successful career in operetta opposite John Hanson and a busy concert schedule. She also appeared in the Brent Walker film of *Iolanthe*.

Caer "Phili" Chicken Breast

with Parma Ham

CHICKEN BREAST FILLED WITH GARLIC AND HERB PHILADELPHIA AND WRAPPED IN PARMA HAM

Ingredients (for 2)

2 chicken breasts (skinless and boneless)
2 dessert spoons of garlic and herb Philadelphia
6 slices of Parma ham

Serve with new potatoes and salad/or asparagus tips and baby sweet corn

Cut a slit in each chicken breast. Start at the thickest part, but don't cut it all the way through to the other side.

Take a dessert spoonful of the garlic and herb Philadelphia and spoon it into the slit in the chicken.

Wrap the slices of Parma ham tightly around the chicken. Place the wrapped chicken breasts in the oven for 20-30 minutes at 180°c / Gas Mark 4-5 until the chicken is cooked through.

If any of the Philadelphia oozes out, just scoop it over the chicken as a sauce.

Enjoy!.

Pamela Field

As Princess Zara in "Utopia Ltd' with husband David Porter as Mr Blushington. David was with the Company from 1972–75

Sir Arthur Sullivan

Christmas day and the cook's unwell ...

Our esteemed composer and co-founder of our feast, found himself with no feast of his own one Christmas! He was due to celebrate with his friends Lord and Lady Russell but his cook was unwell and he sent his staff home.

"Please don't come today – my cook is ill. Come tomorrow. I am having cutlets".

We can only hope that this Director of the Savoy Hotel, with his knowledge of the finest eating establishments and love of good food and fine wine, was adequately prepared for this solitary meal and able to cook it!

Ingredients (Serves 4)

½ oz butter
one small onion- skinned and finely chopped
one medium carrot finely sliced
2 oz lean ham cut into thin strips
4tbsp red wine vinegar
3 tbsp port
1 pint lamb or chicken stock
2 cloves
2 blades of mace
1 bay leaf

4 juniper berries (crushed)
a pinch of dried thyme
2oz finely chopped, cooked ham
1 tbsp cornflour.
8 lamb cutlets French trimmed
20z white bread crumbs
1 beaten egg.

Marilyn Hill Smith

When Marilyn appeared as a Guest Artiste with the New D'Oyly Carte Opera Company in 1990, she was no stranger to G&S having toured the UK, USA and Canada with Donald Adams and Thomas Round in *Gilbert & Sullivan For All*.

She was a Principal Soprano with English National Opera for six years and has also sung with the Royal Opera at Covent Garden, Welsh National Opera, Scottish Opera (including their recording of Bernstein's *Candide*) and with the Canadian and Singapore Companies. Her impressive festival work has taken her to Aldeburgh, Versailles, Rome and Hong Kong whilst her recording catalogue has included work with the New Sadler's Wells Opera (*Ruddigore*, *The Count of Luxembourg* & *Countess Maritza*), *Treasures of Operetta* and solo albums of Ivor Novello, Kalman and Lehár for Chandos, *The Student Prince* for TER and Arthur Sullivan's *The Rose of Persia* for the BBC. She has also been a favourite guest singer for *Friday Night is Music Night* making over 100 appearances over the years.

Marilyn enjoyed great personal success as the Mother Abbess in Andrew Lloyd Webber's production of *The Sound of Music*.

Cutlets Reform

This dish was invented in the 1830's by the French chef Alexis Soyer at the Reform Club in Pall Mall, London. Escoffier also lists the dish in his book *The Complete Guide to the Art of Modern Cookery*.

Method

Sauce: Melt the butter in a medium size saucepan then add the onion,carrot and ham strips. Cook gently until just turning brown. Add the vinegar and port then boil rapidly until almost half the liquid evaporates. Remove the pan from the heat and add the stock, cloves, mace, bay leaf, juniper berries and thyme. Stir well, return to the heat and bring to the boil. Lower the heat and simmer for about 30 mins. Blend the cornflour with about 2 tbsp. water and add to the sauce. Stir well, bring to the boil – stirring continuosly. Simmer until thickened.

Cutlets: Break the egg into a bowl and whisk. Prepare some fresh bread crumbs from white bread, place some plain flour into a flat dish and add some seasoning. (At the Savoy, Chef Escoffier would also add some chopped ham and parsley into the flour).

Dip each cutlet into the seasoned flour, then into the beaten egg and finally into the breadcrumbs, fry in oil until golden brown (around 5 mins each side.) To test if cooked; press each cutlet firmly – no blood should appear. Serve garnished with watercress and with the sauce in a sauceboat; vegetables of choice – perhaps new potatoes, French beans and baby carrots tossed in butter with some chopped parsley.

Chicken à la Carte

Chop 1 large onion and ¼ lb smoked bacon.

Fry together gently in a little butter till soft and golden brown. Set aside.

In little oil, fry 8 large skinless chicken thighs quickly.

Transfer to casserole dish, sprinkle bacon and onion mixture over, season to taste, adding dried herbs and 1 bay leaf, and 6oz sliced mushrooms.

Using same frying pan for flavours, add ¼ pint water and ¼ pint milk, and dissolve 1 chicken stock cube. Thicken this sauce and pour over chicken.

Cook in moderate oven for about an hour and a half.

With good wishes
Marilyn Hill Smith

Dame Bridget D'Oyly Carte D.B.E.

Bridget D'Oyly Carte was born in 1908, the daughter of Rupert D'Oyly Carte and Lady Dorothy Milner Gathorne-Hardy (herself, the daughter of the 2nd Earl of Cranbrooke). At the age of 18 she married her cousin (the 4th Earl of Cranbrook) but the marriage was dissolved five years later, and after resuming her maiden name Bridget worked as assistant to her father at the Savoy.

During the war, she was heavily involved with child welfare in London and dealt with the evacuation of nursery schools. On Rupert's death she assumed control of her father's business interests and the running of the D'Oyly Carte Opera Company. With the lapse of the copyright in 1961 she considered ending the family association with the Savoy Operas, but was persuaded instead to form the D'Oyly Carte Opera Trust, a charitable organization which she endowed with her Company's scenery, costumes, wigs, props, band parts and other assets. The new trust assigned to her the presentation of the operas by the newly-formed Bridget D'Oyly Carte Ltd. of which she was Chairman and Managing Director.

She was also a Director of the Savoy Group, personally taking control of the furnishing and decor departments, and at the time of her death in 1985 was the Company's President and major shareholder thereby keeping a close connection with the Savoy itself. She was also Chairman of Edward Goodyear, the royal florists. The former family seaside home in Devon is now owned by the National Trust, and Dame Bridget spent over thirty years at Shrubs Wood in Buckinghamshire in a house designed by Russian architect Serge Chermayeff. Here she enjoyed her great passion for gardening.

Mary Godfrey and Dame Bridget with the portrait of Isidore Godfrey O.B.E. at the Savoy.

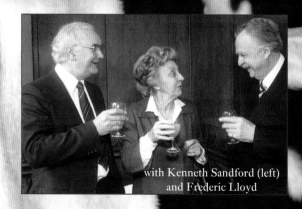

with Kenneth Sandford (left) and Frederic Lloyd

Ingredients

1 kg diced chicken

1 tbsp coriander

1 tsp cardamom

1 tsp clove powder

1 tbsp chili powder

1 tsp black peppercorns

4 cinnamon sticks

2 tsp cumin seeds

2 tsp fenugreek seeds

2 tsp fresh minced ginger

2 tsp turmeric powder and 2tsp mustard powder

2 tsp salt; 2tsp crushed garlic

I cup of vinegar

6 tbsp. vegetable oil

5 bay leaves

2 onions (chopped)

300 ml water

Dame Bridget with Mary Godfrey in the garden of 'Little Saxons', the Godfrey residence in Bosham, West Sussex.
Photograph taken by Isidore Godfrey

Method

Roast the coriander, cardamom, cloves, peppercorns, cinnamon, cumin, fenugreek, ginger and chili powder for about 5 minutes on a low heat in a frying pan.

When done, put these into a blender and add the mustard, salt, garlic, turmeric and vinegar. Add a little water if required.

Marinate the chicken in this sauce for approx. 8 hours in a Pyrex bowl (or any non-metallic container).

Heat the oil and sauté the onions and bay leaves until soft. Remove from heat.

Fry the marinated chicken for a few minutes. Add more oil if required.

Now add the remaining sauce, onion and water.

Stirring well, simmer until the chicken is tender and the curry thickens.

Add salt and chilli if preferred.

Serve with Basmati rice, prepared in the usual way.

Too hot?
"the question is ... will it be hot enough?"

Joyce Perry (Joy Garland)

Joyce Perry (Joy Garland) was in the D'Oyly Carte Chorus from December 1930 until July 1933 when she retired from the stage to marry Dr Hugh Garland. Her closeness to the Company and the Savoy Operas led to the eventual publication of this book. Members of the "New" D'Oyly Carte were happy to meet her at performances in Bournemouth in 1996 and she was a regular and welcome guest at many concerts at Oak Hall Manor in Sussex.

Joyce with Sir Henry Lytton and Muriel Page

Joy's Lamb Curry

Preceded by Dr. Hugh Garland's Gin & Grapefruit Cocktail

Ingredients

2 parts Gin to 5 parts Grapefruit. (Adjust to taste!)

Method

Fill a highball glass with ice; add Gin then freshly squeezed Grapefruit Juice; Stir.

Ingredients

1.25 kg boned shoulder or leg of lamb

¾ cup flour, seasoned

100g butter

2 green apples, peeled, cored, quartered and sliced

2 onions, chopped

1 tomato, quartered

2 cloves garlic, crushed

1-2 tbs curry powder

1¾ cups stock

grated rind and juice of half a lemon

1 ts brown sugar

2 tbs desiccated coconut

2 tbs sultans or raisins

1 tbs flaked almond

6 cups boiled rice, for serving

red capsicum (peppers) or lemon twists, to garnish

Method

Trim lamb of excess fat and cut meat into cubes. Toss in flour and shake off any excess.

Melt butter and fry meat until evenly browned. Remove meat and set aside.

Add apples to pan with onions, tomato, garlic and curry powder. Fry 2-3 minutes and poor off any excess fat. Add stock. Return meat to pan and add remaining ingredients except almonds. Cover and simmer 2 hours, or until meat is tender. Stir in almonds.

Serve lamb curry with boiled rice. Garnish with red peppers or lemon twists.

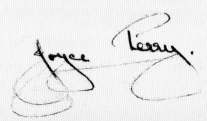

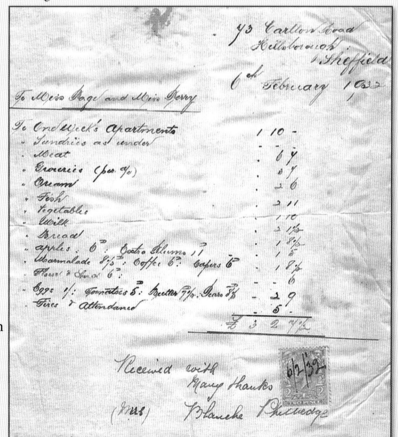

Digs receipt for Joyce and Muriel Page, Sheffield 1932

Michael Rayner

Few voices were more impressive in G&S than that of Michael Rayner. His resonant bass-baritone always made an impact – especially as Captain Corcoran in *H.M.S. Pinafore* and Pish-Tush in *The Mikado* – his recording of this role has not been bettered. He also seemed to relish playing Lieutenant of the Tower, Arac, Sergeant of Police and Counsel in *Trial by Jury*. He had studied at the Birmingham School of Music before joining the WNO Opera For All troupe where he sang Sharpless in *Madam Butterfly*, Figaro in *The Barber of Seville* and Frank in *Die Fledermaus*. During his D'Oyly Carte career (1971-79) he also sang in the Centenary revivals of *Utopia Ltd* and *The Grand Duke*, both of which he recorded for Decca.

Mike's Mild & Creamy Chicken Curry

Ingredients

Two medium to large onions

4 medium sized chicken breasts

2 large red chillies deseeded

1 large green chilli deseeded

5/6 cloves garlic

2 inch piece ginger

2 teaspoon whole cumin seeds

2 teaspoon whole fenugreek seeds

Tablespoon sugar or to taste

1-2 tablespoon mild curry powder or to taste

1 tin coconut milk

1-2 bananas

4 tablespoons vegetable or sunflower oil

Salt to taste

One of the traditional "Last Night" performances sees Michael as the Sergeant of Police helping Colin Wright (Nanki-Poo) clean up after a visit by the Mikado and his horse!

Method

Heat the oil in a heavy based pan or wok on a high heat.

Add the cumin and fenugreek seeds to the hot oil and fry for 30/45 seconds.

Turn down the heat and add the chopped chicken pieces and gently seal but do not brown them.

Finely chop the chillies with garlic and ginger (I use a small coffee grinder)

Add salt, chilli mixture, garlic and ginger and sugar to the chicken in the pan, stir and cook for a further minute or two stirring all the time.

Add the coconut milk, stir and cover the pan and simmer gently until the chicken is cooked, about 45 mins. After cooking, if the sauce is too thin, I thicken it with dessicated coconut. Add the bananas.

"I find that no two curries are the same and I often experiment and try different things like using plain yoghurt or a mixture of cream and yoghurt. If you are using yoghurt make sure to add a teaspoon of corn flour to avoid the curry splitting. I sometimes add pineapple chunks with the bananas."

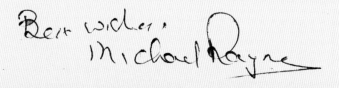

Gareth Jones

Gareth's connection with D'Oyly Carte began in 1973 and over the years he would play all of the baritone roles either in his own right or, initially, as understudy to Kenneth Sandford and Michael Rayner. In the re-formed Company of 1988, along with Gillian Knight, Vivian Tierney and Jill Pert, he became one of the few artistes to make the transition into the new era of D'Oyly Carte production. With him came all his customary style, finesse and respect for the work of the original Company.

His successes included the new non G&S ventures, *Orpheus in the Underworld*, *La Vie Parisienne* and *The Count of Luxembourg*, and his exemplary singing has been enjoyed on several D'Oyly Carte recordings over the years, notably *Cox and Box* and *Orpheus*.

A versatile actor with a love of the English language, he appeared in the West End (including *La Cage aux Folles* and *The Phantom of the Opera*) and sang his signature repertoire with the Carl Rosa Company, Opera della Luna and at the Buxton International G&S Festival with the Gilbert and Sullivan Opera Company. He also had an encyclopaedic knowledge of the world of comedy and his skills as a backstage raconteur would lift the mood of many Mikado matinees!!

Colleagues and friends were stunned by his premature death in 2010.

Gazza's Beef Curry

Ingredients

2lbs Beef or Mince
1 small onion;
4 cloves of garlic
1 tsp ground cumin
5 tsp curry powder
1 tbsp tomato paste
4 potatoes
Salt to taste

In *La Vie Parisienne* with Richard Suart

Method

If not using minced beef, cut the beef into small chunks and rinse under the tap.

Dice the onion and garlic together, or grate if preferred.

Put oil in a pressure cooker (medium).

Add the onion and garlic and allow to fry. Now add the curry powder and cumin, stirring all the time for around 4 minutes.

Add the meat to the mixture and season with salt. Loosely cover the pressure cooker and leave until the meat is cooked (still stirring occasionally) and add the water to cover the meat as required.

Leave for up to 7 minutes and check the tenderness of the meat as a guide.

Add the potatoes and cook until ready.

Serve with rice.

113

John Fryatt

John was born in York and joined the D'Oyly Carte Chorus in 1952 playing minor roles. Within two years he was cast as Hilarion in the revival of *Princess Ida* and as Defendant in *Trial by Jury* as well as substituting, on occasion, as Nanki-Poo, Frederic and Ralph Rackstraw. On leaving the company in 1959, he joined the Sadler's Wells Opera and soon enjoyed much success in comedy character roles, notably in Wendy Toye's wonderful productions of *Orpheus in the Underworld*, *La Belle Helene* and *La Vie Parisienne*. However, his achievements went way beyond the boundaries of operetta and his portrayal of Don Basilio in *The Marriage of Figaro* was seen at English National Opera, Glyndebourne and in opera houses throughout the USA and Europe. He also sang the role on Daniel Barrenboim's 1977 recording opposite Sir Geraint Evans and Dietrich Fischer-Dieskau. John performed in *The Rake's Progress* at Rome Opera, *Porgy and Bess* at Carnegie Hall, *Madam Butterfly* in Amsterdam and in many productions at the Royal Opera House.

Stanley Parker

Stanley H. Parker was with the D'Oyly Carte management from 1913–1960. He was Secretary, Treasurer and subsequently, confidante to Rupert D'Oyly Carte, having previously worked as an office-boy at the Savoy Hotel. He remained in the same job when Rupert's daughter Bridget took over the Company in 1948 after her father's death. He was there for the landmark 1919 season at the Princes Theatre, personally dealt with the temporary disbandment of the opera company on the outbreak of the second world war in 1939, and liaised between Bridget D'Oyly Carte and Charles Mackerras in the preparation of the ballet suite *Pineapple Poll*. Stanley, affectionately known as "Pickwick" to his colleagues, died on September 20th 1960, a few months before the formation of the D'Oyly Carte Opera Trust and the expiration of the G&S Copyright. His son Peter remains an invaluable source of information and anecdote and a loyal supporter of performances of the Savoy Operas.

Stanley (centre) with, left to right, Bruce Worsley, Peter Parker, Fisher Morgan, Leonard Osborn, Frederic Lloyd, Dr. Budd (Buddy) Peter Pratt, Alan Styler, Bert Newby, Neville Griffiths and Donald Adams. Alan is holding the golf-cup sponsored by Dr. Budd.

Roast Duck

Ingredients

1 whole duck (about 2.25 kg)

2 tsp salt

2 tsp paprika

1 tsp black pepper

110g melted butter

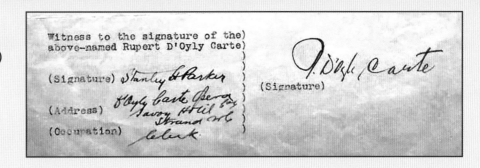

Method

1. Preheat the oven to 190C or Gas mark 5

2. Rub the paprika, salt and pepper into the duck skin. Place in a roasting tin

3. Roast in the oven for an hour

4. Baste with half the melted butter and roast for a further 45 minutes.

5. Baste with the rest of the butter and roast for another 15 minutes. Remove when golden brown.

Duck with Orange

Ingredients

2 duck breast fillets (with the skin)

2 passion fruits

1 tbsp. olive oil

1 garlic clove

The juice of two oranges

1 tbsp. of light brown sugar

1 tbsp. of soy sauce

Method

Score the skin of the duck breasts in a diamond pattern

Cut the passion fruits in half and scoop out into a small dish

Heat the oil (not too hot) in a pan and cook the duck breasts (with the skin facing down) for about 6 minutes until nice and brown. Turn them over and repeat. Check that the meat is tender. Place on a warm plate for now.

Drain off the duck fat but save about a tbsp. full and use it to cook the garlic until it starts to brown. Add the passion fruit, orange juice, soy sauce and sugar, stirring all the time. Boil for about 7-10 minutes until it reduces by about two thirds.

Season and add the remaining juices from the duck.

Sieve the sauce and spread over and around the meat as required.

Can be served with a salad, rice or both!!

Kathleen Parkhurst

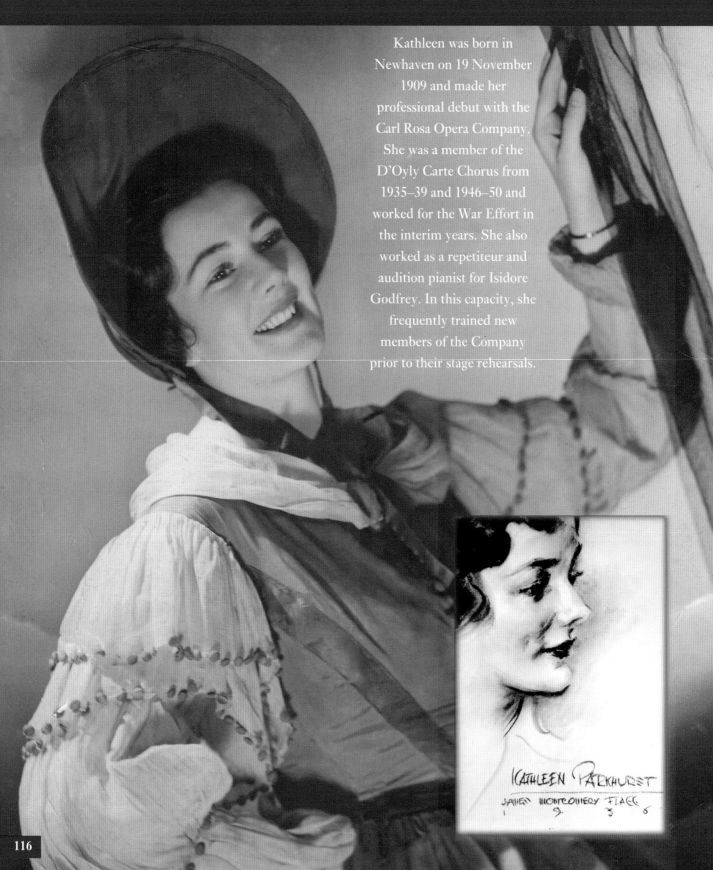

Kathleen was born in Newhaven on 19 November 1909 and made her professional debut with the Carl Rosa Opera Company. She was a member of the D'Oyly Carte Chorus from 1935–39 and 1946–50 and worked for the War Effort in the interim years. She also worked as a repetiteur and audition pianist for Isidore Godfrey. In this capacity, she frequently trained new members of the Company prior to their stage rehearsals.

Yorkshire Pudding

Yorkshire Pudding.

Put two tablespoons of flour into a basin, pinch of salt and stir. break two new laid eggs and stir. carefully add a quarter of a pint of milk and beat for ten minutes. leave to stand for one hour, or longer. Place in hot greased pie dish, and bake in hot oven for. 15 minutes.

Kathleen

Kathleen (centre) making-up for *Iolanthe* in the dressing
room assigned to "small-part" artistes

Alan Styler

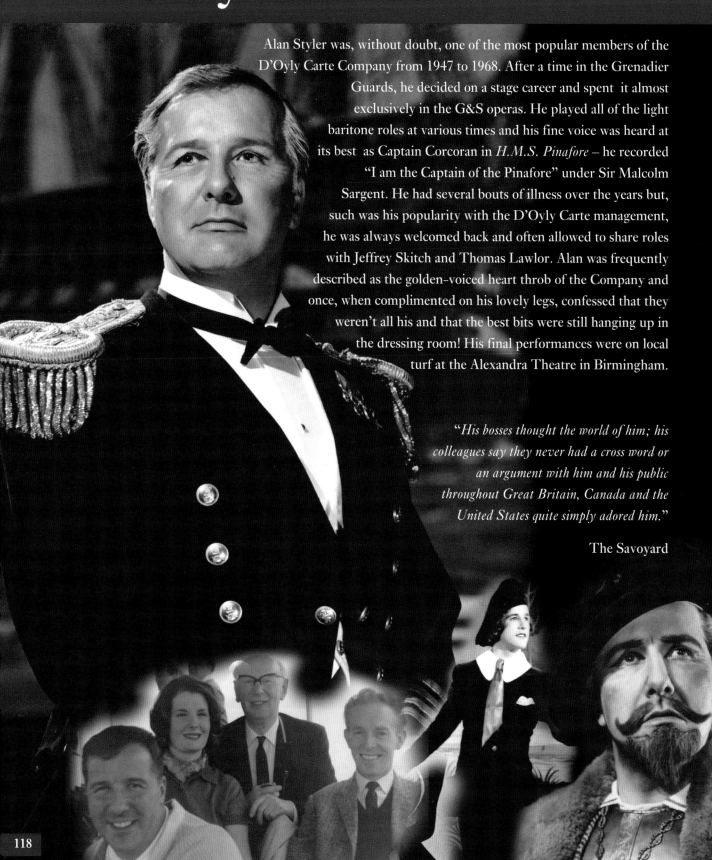

Alan Styler was, without doubt, one of the most popular members of the D'Oyly Carte Company from 1947 to 1968. After a time in the Grenadier Guards, he decided on a stage career and spent it almost exclusively in the G&S operas. He played all of the light baritone roles at various times and his fine voice was heard at its best as Captain Corcoran in *H.M.S. Pinafore* – he recorded "I am the Captain of the Pinafore" under Sir Malcolm Sargent. He had several bouts of illness over the years but, such was his popularity with the D'Oyly Carte management, he was always welcomed back and often allowed to share roles with Jeffrey Skitch and Thomas Lawlor. Alan was frequently described as the golden-voiced heart throb of the Company and once, when complimented on his lovely legs, confessed that they weren't all his and that the best bits were still hanging up in the dressing room! His final performances were on local turf at the Alexandra Theatre in Birmingham.

"His bosses thought the world of him; his colleagues say they never had a cross word or an argument with him and his public throughout Great Britain, Canada and the United States quite simply adored him."

The Savoyard

Alan's beloved "Gippo" Gravy

"Gippo" is army slang for gravy.

This recipe was supplied by Alan's wife, Vera Ryan who was with the Company from 1959–61 and 1966–67

Ingredients (Serves 4)

3/4 pint of water

1 stock cube (beef or chicken)

White pepper

1tsp Marmite

1tbsp white plain flour

1tbsp fat from the meat or the chicken

Method

The D'Oyly Carte heart throb

Heat the water until the cube has dissolved. Add the pepper, fat and Marmite. Mix the flour into a smooth paste with a little cold water and slowly add to the stock and bring to the boil, stirring constantly.

The secret of Alan's shapely legs revealed for the first time

"And there it is! Alan used to cook a wonderful dinner for a few friends and then promptly fall asleep at the table once he had eaten it. I was then left to entertain our guests.

Warmest good wishes,

Vera"

119

*"Nonsense, yes perhaps – but oh,
what precious nonsense."*
Lady Angela: Patience.

> *"Then a sentimental passion of a vegetable fashion must excite your languid spleen ... an attachment à la Plato for a bashful young potato, or a not-too-French French bean!"*
> Reginald Bunthorne: *Patience*.

Sir Henry Lytton on tour –
another gem from
Joyce Perry's photo album.

VEGETARIAN

Leslie Rands and family

Leslie Rands is remembered for his classic good looks and fine baritone voice. Born in Chichester, he was a chorister at the cathedral before joining the D'Oyly Carte in 1925. So precise was his diction, he could "*make the word 'Leeds' sound like it had two syllables*" (quote from Donald Adams) and his many skills included dazzling fan work as Pish-Tush in *The Mikado*.

He was a Guest Artist on the 1949 recording of *H.M.S. Pinafore* and appeared in his home town alongside his wife Marjorie Eyre, Anne Ziegler and Webster Booth in a charity production of *Merrie England* in 1952. He died in 1972.

The "Randsowian" Spinach Cream.

1 lb. Spinach   1 Tablespoonful cream.

2 Tomatos.   1 oz. Butter,

Brown Bread.

Boil the spinach; pass it through a sieve; add the cream & heat them up together. Melt the butter in a stew pan; add the mixture; heat until it gets fairly firm. Serve on brown bread cut in thick rounds. Garnish with slices of tomatos & thick of Leslie, Marjorie + Ian.

Jane Metcalfe

Jane studied at the Royal College of Music and in Geneva, after winning the Sir Thomas Beecham Scholarship. She sang with Scottish Opera, Glyndebourne and the Ambrosian Opera Chorus, prior to joining the D'Oyly Carte in 1975, as Principal Mezzo-Soprano. She impressed immediately with her fine voice and enjoyed much success as Lady Angela, Iolanthe, Pitti-Sing, Phoebe, Tessa, Melissa and Mad Margaret. She also recorded the role of Lisa in *The Grand Duke*. She left the Company in 1979 and enjoyed a fruitful concert career before concentrating on teaching, notably at the Guildhall School of Music.

Shepherdess Pie

Ingredients

For the lentil sauce

50g butter
2 onions, chopped, 4 carrots, diced, 1 head of celery, chopped
4 garlic cloves, finely chopped
200g pack chestnut mushrooms, sliced (fresh mushrooms better)
2 bay leaves
I tbsp dried thyme
500g pack dried green lentils
100ml red wine (optional)
1.7 litres vegetable stock
3 tbsps tomato puree

"Food for joyous laughter..."
Jane Rehdeye

For the topping

2kg floury potatoes, such as King Edwards
85g butter, 100ml milk, 50g cheddar, grated

Method

1. To make the sauce, heat the butter in a pan, and then gently fry the onions, carrots, celery and garlic for 15 mins until soft and golden. Turn up the heat, add the mushrooms, and then cook for 4 mins more. Stir in the herbs, and then add the lentils. Pour over the wine and stock – it's important that you do not season with salt at this stage. Simmer for 40–50 mins until the lentils are very soft. Now season to taste, take off the heat, and then stir in the tomato puree.
2. While the lentils are cooking, tip the potatoes into a pan of water and then boil for about 15 mins until tender. Drain well, mash with the butter and milk and then season with salt and pepper.
3. To assemble the pies, divide the lentil mixture between all the dishes that you are using and then top with mash. Scatter over the cheese and freeze for up to two months or if eating that day, heat oven to 190C/fan 170C/gas 5 and then bake for 30 mins until the topping is golden.

Jon Ellison

It would be hard to find a more popular Savoyard, on or off stage, than Jon Ellison. His performance energy and enthusiasm was infectious and to his many friends and colleagues he was warm, considerate and a consummate professional. In the D'Oyly Carte, he took the role of "supporting artiste" to the level of a star principal and we are indeed fortunate that his classic portrayal of the Boatswain in *H.M.S. Pinafore* is safely secured on the 1970 recording. Who else could give the waiter in *The Gondoliers* such finesse and make lasting impressions as Bunthorne's solicitor, Second Citizen in *Yeomen* and Ben Hashbaz; his Samuel in *Pirates* was a great partner for John Ayldon's Pirate King. He was spurred on to audition after winning a prize at the Llangollen International Eisteddfod and sang for Isidore Godfrey at the Theatre Royal Birmingham. On 1 September 1953, the day of Darrell Fancourt's funeral, he joined the Company and stayed until 1979 (except for a short spell in pantomime and *The Black & White Minstrel Show*).

Vegetarian Goulash

Ingredients

1x300g pack Quorn pieces

2 heaped teaspoons paprika

¼ –½ teaspoon chilli powder (to taste)

Salt and ground black pepper

1 small red and 1 small green pepper

60g (2 oz.) sliced mushrooms

1 chopped onion

1x300g can condensed tomato soup (together with vegetable stock and a little milk to dilute)

1 tablespoon sunflower oil

Method

In a frying pan lightly sauté chopped onion and Quorn pieces until softened. Add the chopped peppers and mushrooms and then cook a further 5 mins. Meantime mix the spices together and sprinkle over the Quorn mixture. Heat diluted soup to boiling. Transfer all to a casserole dish and continue cooking in a moderate oven for 30 mins. Be generous with the paprika as it is high in Vitamin C. Meat eaters have shared this meal with us, quite convinced that they were eating chicken or pork. Serve with creamed potatoes or rice and a green vegetable.

Jon Elli

Peggy O'Brien, Maisie Baxter
and Muriel Dickson

Maisie Baxter. Joined the D'Oyly Carte Opera Company in July 1929 as a chorister. With the sudden death of Bertha Lewis, she played Queen of the Fairies, Lady Blanche, Dame Carruthers and the Duchess of Plaza-Toro until Dorothy Gill became Principal Contralto. She subsequently played Kate (*Pirates*), Lady Saphir, Leila and Chloe in *Princess Ida* until leaving the Company in 1935.

Peggy O'Brien. A member of the D'Oyly Carte Chorus from 1926–28 and 1929–35, she made occasional appearances in both soprano and mezzo roles including Lady Ella, Casilda, Tessa and Pitti-Sing.

Sunday morning Train Call with Maisie (right), Muriel and Sir Henry Lytton

"MY GREATEST AMBITION—SING AT COVENT GARDEN"

NEW YORK ACCLAIMS A BRITISH SINGER

By A Special Correspondent

BY TRANSATLANTIC TELEPHONE LAST NIGHT THE SUNDAY DISPATCH CONGRATULATED MISS MURIEL DICKSON, PRETTY BLONDE SOPRANO OF THE D'OYLY CARTE OPERA COMPANY ON HER REMARKABLE TRIUMPH OF A FEW HOURS PREVIOUSLY, WHEN HUNDREDS OF EXCITED NEW YORKERS RUSHED ON THE STAGE OF THE METROPOLITAN OPERA HOUSE TO ACCLAIM HER AFTER HER DEBUT IN OPERA.

Muriel Dickson

Cheese Soufflé and Tomatoes with Cheese Stuffing

Washington, New Hampshire

Cheese Soufflé

3 tablespoons Tapioca
1 teaspoon salt
1 cup milk
1 cup grated cheese
3 egg-yolks (beaten until thick & lemon-coloured).
3 egg-whites stiffly beaten.

Combine Tapioca salt and milk in top of double boiler. Place over rapidly boiling water, bring to scalding point (allow 3 to 5 minutes) and cook 5 minutes, stirring frequently. Add cheese & stir until melted. Remove from boiling water;

cool slightly. Add egg-yolks and mix well. Fold in egg-whites. Turn into greased baking dish. Place in pan of hot water; bake in moderate oven (350°F.) 50 minutes, or until firm.   Serves 6.
(When made with Tapioca, and properly baked, soufflés do not fall but stay tender, moist & light while being served.)

Muriel Dickson

Tomatoes with Cheese Stuffing.

6. firm Tomatoes.   2 tablespoonfuls
6 rounds of toast.   parmesan cheese.
2 tablespoonfuls bread ½ oz. butter.
   - crumbs.   chopped parsley.
Choose Tomatoes of equal size.
Cut a small round from the top of each & scoop out the pulp.
Mix the Stuffing, moisten with tomato pulp & mix well. Refill tomato cases, sprinkle a few crumbs or grated cheese & place a piece of butter on each. Bake in a greased tin in a moderate oven 15-20 mins. Serve on rounds of buttered toast & garnish with parsley.
To be eaten in moderation!!
Maisie.

Cauliflower - au - Gratin.

1 large cauliflower
½ lb grated cheese
2 oz bread crumbs.

Boil cauliflower for about twenty minutes — then strain and cut into sections.   Butter a pie dish, and put alternate layers of cauliflower, grated cheese, and bread crumbs. Season to taste.   Cook in warm oven for about thirty minutes — until browned on top.
Peggy O'Brien

129

Donald Adams

After his education at the Bristol Cathedral School and early work with the BBC Repertory Company, Great Yarmouth Rep, pantomime and a stint as a washerwoman with *Old Mother Riley* (Arthur Lucan), Donald joined the D'Oyly Carte Opera Company in 1951. After further vocal work (on the advice of Isidore Godfrey) he was ready to take over from Darrell Fancourt in 1953 and was destined to become one of the towering personalities of the Company until he left in 1969. He was a truly unforgettable Pirate King, *Mikado*, Sir Roderic and Colonel Calverley but equally unmissable in his other roles. Donald was half of the *Gilbert & Sullivan For All* dynamic duo (with Thomas Round), and enjoyed an operatic renaissance which took him to the Royal Opera House, Welsh National Opera, English National Opera, Glyndeboure, Chicago, Los Angeles, Amsterdam and Canadian Opera. He triumphed as Baron Ochs in *Der Rosenkavalier*, Dolittle in *My Fair Lady* and in Britten's *A Midsummer Night's Dream* in which opera he was contracted to appear at the New York Met. It was an engagement he was unable to keep: on the night of his death, the D'Oyly Carte performance of *The Mikado* was dedicated to his treasured memory.

Don's Traditional Cheese 'n' Onion Pie

Ingredients

1 lb. 2 oz. (500g) ready-made short crust pastry

1 tbsp. flour for dusting

9 oz. (250g) of your favourite cheddar

3 medium sized onions

1 oz. (30g) butter

2 large eggs

Ground black pepper

1 tbsp. milk

Snapshot of Donald's wife, Muriel Harding in *H.M.S. Pinafore.*

Method

Defrost the pastry; chop the onions; grate the cheese.

Divide the pastry into two: 1) two thirds 2) one third.

Pre-heat the oven to 180C / Gas Mark 4; grease the pie dish in readiness.

Break the eggs into a bowl and whisk.

Place the butter in a heated pan, add the onions and season with the pepper. Simmer gently and stir.

Roll out the larger portion of pastry and cover the dish allowing the pastry to hang over the sides. Use a fork to make small holes in the pastry base.

Let the onions cool in a bowl while you roll out the remaining pastry to a large enough size to make the lid to the dish.

Mix the onion with the cheese and season with more pepper; add to the pastry case. Pour over the eggs.

Brush milk over the pastry lid and place over the pie with the brushed side down.

Pinch the edges of the pastry; remove the surplus, cut a couple of holes in the top, brush with the milk. Cook for 45 minutes

"Soft serenading" with Bert Newby

Take care

Donald

Ivor Emmanuel

Ivor Emmanuel was orphaned during the Second World War and started work down the coal mines around Port Talbot. He loved music and auditioned unsuccessfully for the D'Oyly Carte in 1947; his friend, film star Richard Burton, arranged an audition for the original West End production of *Oklahoma* and his career was launched. His next audition for Bridget D'Oyly Carte resulted in an 18 month contract as chorister, Associate in *Trial by Jury* and Luiz in *The Gondoliers* which he shared with Eric Thornton and Henry Goodier.

He left the Company to join the London cast of *South Pacific*, followed by *The King and I*, *Finian's Rainbow* and *Damn Yankees*, became a star of the radio series *Gwlad Y Gan* (Land of Song) and sang in the first televised Royal Variety Performance. On Broadway he appeared in *A Time For Singing* with Tessie O'Shea and made a brief return to Gilbert and Sullivan in a recording of *The Pirates of Penzance* with Martyn Green. Ivor's film work included the role of Private Owen in *Zulu*.

His many recordings are still available today.

Ivor retired to Spain in 1982 where he lived until his death in 2007.

Ivor's Best Welsh Rarebit

Ingredients

3 tbsp. Guinness
1 tsp mustard powder
30g butter
1 tsp Worcestershire sauce
175g grated Welsh cheese
Bread

Method

Mix a small portion of Guinness with the mustard powder in a pan and stir until it becomes a paste.

Add the remainder of the Guinness, butter and Worcestershire sauce. Heat gently until the butter melts.

Add the grated cheese and stir. The mix will melt but don't let it boil.

Season to taste; remove from the heat and allow to cool down a little.

Toast the bread (both sides) under the grill.

Beat the egg yolks into the cheese mixture and when smooth, layer onto the toast.

Continue to grill until golden.

D'Oyly Carte supporter Tessie O'Shea backstage with Bruce Worsley

133

Beatrice Elburn

Ena Martin

Ena was a member of the D'Oyly Carte from 1929–34 and 1935-38. From 1932–39 she was married to Company bass-baritone Richard Walker.

Beatrice Elburn sang with the Company from 1925-1930; initially she played minor roles but for a while was Principal Soubrette when Aileen Davies left in 1928. These included Mad Margaret, Iolanthe and Tessa until Marjorie Eyre and Nellie Briercliffe took over as principal artistes leaving Beatrice with the less fulfilling parts of Leila, Peep-Bo and Vittoria. She left the Company in 1930 to appear in *The Fountain of Youth* at the Lyric, Hammersmith, and the West End productions of *Music in the Air* and Noel Coward's *Conversation Piece*.

Kedgeree !

Any fish according to amount required.

Boil & put through a sieve with butter, pepper & salt. Quarter of a pound of rice boiled dry. One hard boiled egg.

method:- Cut the white of egg in small pieces, mix with fish. put in a saucepan with butter & two tablespoonfuls of milk, stir into a cream, put on the dish encircled with rice, grate the yolk over & eat with toast.

Betty.

Short Pastry.

1/2 lb flour.
1/4 " Lard.
2 oz butter
1 Tablespoonful Castor sugar
Pinch of salt
Splash lemon juice.

Mix lard & butter well into flour, then add sugar & salt. Stir in enough water, drop by drop to make mixture firm, (not moist). Roll out on well floured board two or three times. Cut into shape for pie or tarts as desired.

Eva Martin.

Elsie Griffin

Born in Bristol in 1895, Elsie was a recording artist before joining the D'Oyly Carte, enjoying notable success with the hit songs *Danny Boy* and *Roses of Picardy*. From 1919–27 she was the Company's popular Principal Soprano and in 1923 married Ivan Menzies who at the time was understudy to the "Grossmith" roles and would later achieve success in Australia.

She was one of the few D'Oyly Carte artists chosen to sing on the early HMV recordings of the operas, and after leaving the Company in 1927, returned three times as a Guest Artist winning the accolade "Best British Gramophone Solo" in 1929 for her singing of "Poor Wandering One". Further success came in oratorio, BBC broadcasts, UK and South African tours and three years as a Principal with the Carl Rosa Opera Company. She and Ivan toured the world in *The Vanishing Island* – a Moral Re-Armament musical – and in 1975 made their final appearance with the D'Oyly Carte Opera Company in the Savoy Centennial performance of *Trial by Jury* joining other former company stars in the jury box.

Elsie died in 1989.

"... secure coloratura and bell-like tone"
New York Times

"... deliciously fresh and effortless singing ... with trills that would not discredit the great Galli-Curci herself."
Gramophone Magazine

The blue plaque unveiled in Elsie's honour at St. Michael's on the Mount Primary School, Bristol.

Elsie Griffin
1895 - 1989

International opera singer

Principal soprano with D'Oyly Carte Opera Company. Popularised 'Danny Boy' and 'Roses of Picardy'

Attended this school and lived nearby

LONDON HIPPODROME

Chairman: PRINCE LITTLER   Managing Director: VAL PARNELL

230 PERFORMANCES IN FOUR CONTINENTS
London   Premiere

THE VANISHING ISLAND

A MUSICAL PLAY

by Peter Howard & Cecil Broadhurst   Directed by Lewis Allen

with REGINALD OWEN   IVAN MENZIES

ELSIE GRIFFIN   LELAND HOLLAND   JANE WAX

Presented by

MORAL RE-ARMAMENT

" An amazing musical spectacle of an absolutely new type " —*Paris Presse*

" It portrays an ideology which can unite East and West " —*Berlingske Tidende (Copenhagen)*

Commencing MAY 28th   EVENINGS at 7.30 p.m.
Matinees: Wednesday, 30th MAY and Saturday, 2nd JUNE at 2.30

Admission Free by Ticket Only Apply BOX OFFICE Telephone: GERrard 3272

Rub 1 tablespoon butter and 1 desertspoon lard into 1lb. flour with the tips of the fingers, then add 1 teaspoon carbonate of soda, 2 small teaspoons cream of tartar, ¼ teaspoon salt, 1 dessertspoon of caster sugar, and about 2 cups sweet milk.

Mix whole into soft dough with a wooden spoon, then turn out onto a floured board, knead as little as possible, roll out roughly and cut in rounds with a cutter or tumbler. Put on a greased tin, brush over with beaten egg, and bake in a very hot oven for about 10 minutes. When baked, split, butter, and serve hot.

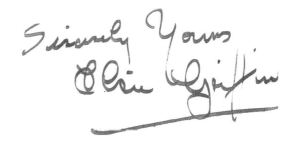

Sincerly Yours
Elsie Griffin

Tea-Cup Brindisi

"Eat, drink and be gay,
Banish all worry and sorrow,
Laugh gaily to-day,
Weep, if you're sorry tomorrow!
Come, pass the cup round –
I will go bail for the liquor;
It's strong, I'll be bound,
For it was brewed by the vicar."

The Sorcerer

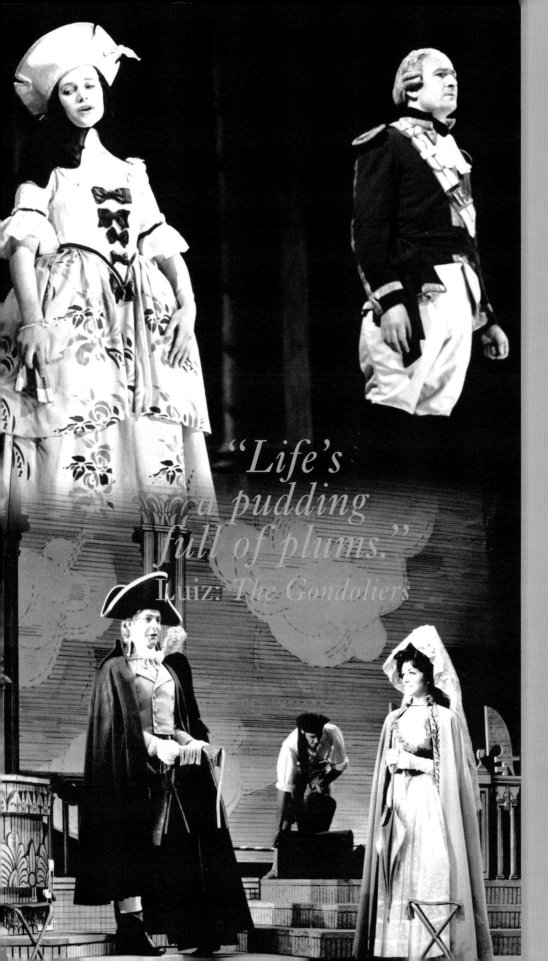

"*Life's
a pudding
full of plums.*"
Luiz: The Gondoliers

139

Dorothy Gill

Made her debut as Principal Contralto of the D'Oyly Carte in Brighton on 3 August 1931 after a varied career which had included a spell entertaining the troops during the First World War. She soon became very popular with D'Oyly Carte audiences and was renowned for her rich voice, impeccable diction and good humour.

Her popularity was such that followers in New York petitioned Rupert D'Oyly Carte when it was announced that she was leaving the Company and would not be part of the 1936 USA tour.

Fromage à la Creme

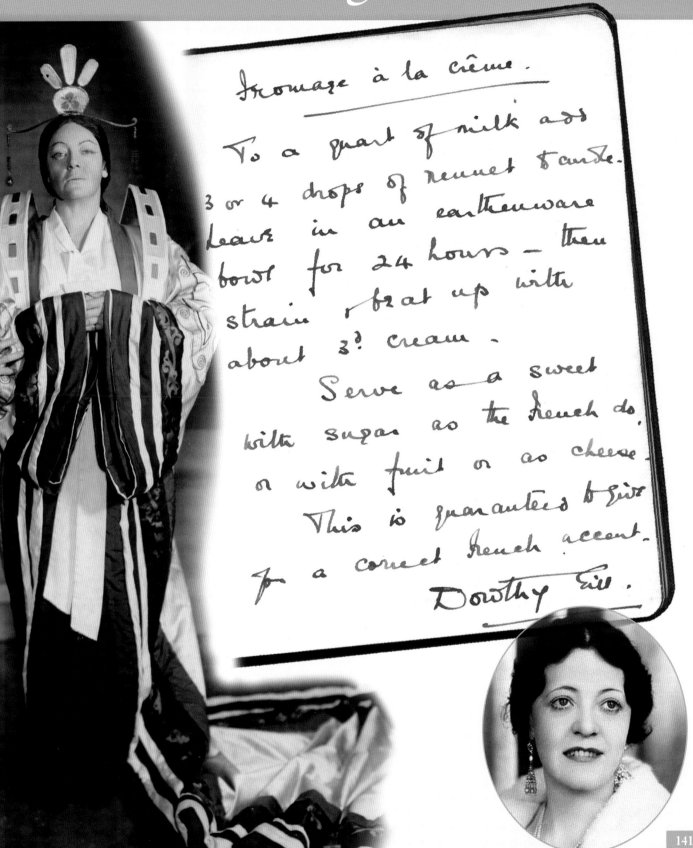

Fromage à la crème.

To a quart of milk add 3 or 4 drops of rennet & curdle. Leave in an earthenware bowl for 24 hours — then strain & beat up with about 3? cream.

Serve as a sweet with sugar as the French do, or with fruit or as cheese.

This is guaranteed to give you a correct French accent.

Dorothy Gill.

Helen Roberts

Helen was born in Cleethorpes in 1912 but spent many years growing up in Italy, where, after training at the Royal Academy in London, she sang Norina in *Don Pasquale* with the Milan Opera Company. In the UK she sang in Offenbach's *The Tales of Hoffman* and at Glyndebourne. She was Principal Soprano with the D'Oyly Carte Opera Company from 1938 staying for 10 years. In 1944, she married Richard Walker and together, they appeared with the J.C. Williamson Company in Australia, toured in *My Fair Lady*, in which she played Mrs Eynsford Hill and gave numerous concerts in the USA, during which time President Eisenhower invited them to sing at his pre-inauguration party. After Richard died, Helen returned to England and was Guest of Honour at the G&S Gala organised by Melvyn Tarran at The Hawth Theatre in Crawley in aid of Great Ormond Street Hospital. She died in December 2010.

Easy Ice Cream

Accompanied by Melvyn Tarran, Helen is reunited with Thomas Round at Oak Hall.

1 cup of cream
3 tablespoons sugar
3 whites of egg
½ teaspoon of vanilla

Whip whites of egg & mix with sugar & vanilla. Whip cream, & mix with above. Place in freezing tray at cold temperature & leave for 2 hours. Do not stir til is ready to eat.

1 Alternative flavours.
2 Chopped nuts & cherries
3 Chocolate chips
4 Finely sliced pineapple

This recipe was given to me in Australia by our hostess on a large cattle station while we were touring it outback with our G&S concert

Helen Roberts

After Melvyn's triumphant G&S Gala at the Hawth Theatre in Crawley, Helen gives David Steadman her observations on the performance!

Thomas Round

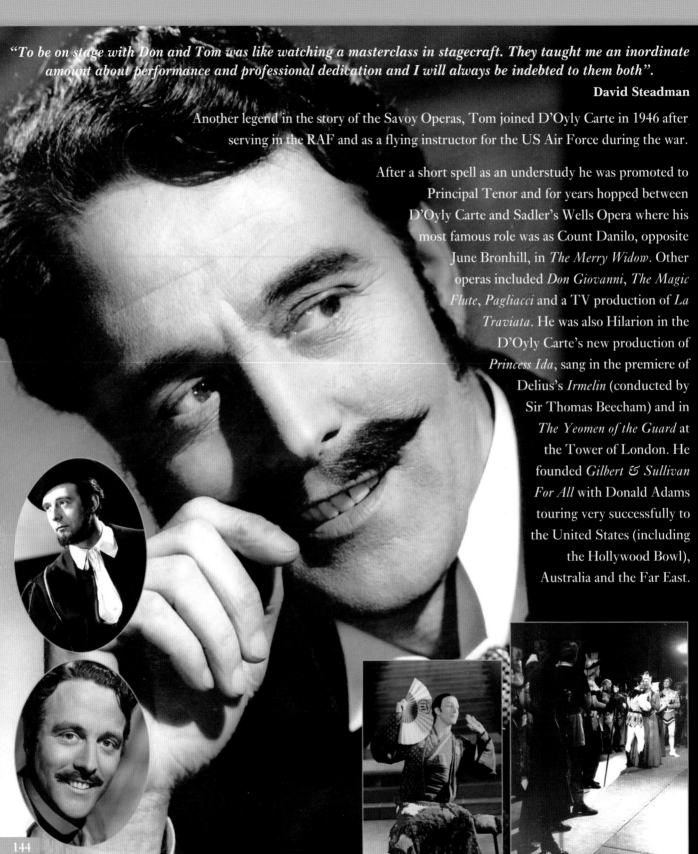

"To be on stage with Don and Tom was like watching a masterclass in stagecraft. They taught me an inordinate amount about performance and professional dedication and I will always be indebted to them both".

David Steadman

Another legend in the story of the Savoy Operas, Tom joined D'Oyly Carte in 1946 after serving in the RAF and as a flying instructor for the US Air Force during the war.

After a short spell as an understudy he was promoted to Principal Tenor and for years hopped between D'Oyly Carte and Sadler's Wells Opera where his most famous role was as Count Danilo, opposite June Bronhill, in *The Merry Widow*. Other operas included *Don Giovanni*, *The Magic Flute*, *Pagliacci* and a TV production of *La Traviata*. He was also Hilarion in the D'Oyly Carte's new production of *Princess Ida*, sang in the premiere of Delius's *Irmelin* (conducted by Sir Thomas Beecham) and in *The Yeomen of the Guard* at the Tower of London. He founded *Gilbert & Sullivan For All* with Donald Adams touring very successfully to the United States (including the Hollywood Bowl), Australia and the Far East.

Marshmallow Banana Pie

Ingredients

Biscuit Crumb base:
½ lb. Digestive Biscuits
4 Level Tablespoons of Golden Syrup
3 oz. Margarine or Butter

Method

Crush biscuits between two sheets of greaseproof paper.
Measure Syrup carefully (level off spoon with back of knife making sure there is none on the underside).
Melt butter (or margarine) and syrup slowly in saucepan.
Stir in crushed biscuits, mix well and press into shallow Pyrex Dish.
Place in Refrigerator until set.

Filling

Cut bananas into slices and cover biscuit base.
Cover bananas with a tin of custard (or make your own recipe custard).
Cover custard with marshmallows.
Place under grill to brown and melt the marshmallows.
Allow to cool. Place in refrigerator until cold.
Serve from base of dish or loose bottomed tin.

31ˢᵗ August. 2001.

Melvyn Tarran Esq.,
Oak Hall Manoʳ.

Dear Melvyn,

Re your proposed "Gilbert and Sullivan Cook Book"

During my first American Tour with The D'Oyly Carte Opera Coy. in 1947/48 we played in Boston for one month, after a four month season in New York.
In New York we met a young lady called Mary Smith, whose home was in Cambridge, Massachusetts, on the outskirts of boston. At that time Mary was the Artistic Secretary of The Boston Symphony Orchestra.
My wife Alice and my 5yr. old son Ellis were with me on the Tour and I asked Mary if she knew of an Apartment Hotel in Boston where we could stay for the month. Mary contacted her mother in Cambridge who found us an apartment in The Commander Hotel in Cambridge. The family are direct descendants of the American Poet, Henry Wadsworth Longfellow. We became, and still are, very good friends.
During a dinner at their home, we were served a Dessert by Mrs Smith and her daughter Francis, which has been a favourite of mine through all these years. It is very simple, very fattening and very delicious.

Thomas Round

Gillian Knight, Tom, Valerie Masterson, Michael Wakeham and David Steadman arrive at Jersey Airport for the final *Gilbert & Sullivan For All* concert, rescheduled as a Farewell Tribute to the late Donald Adams.

145

Gillian Humphreys O.B.E.

Gillian studied singing with Dame Eva Turner and made her G&S debut in the famous productions by Sir Tyrone Guthrie. She then joined the D'Oyly Carte Opera Company as a Principal, and later appeared at Glyndebourne and with the Welsh National Opera. She sang with Nelson Riddle and the California Pops, made numerous television appearances with many of Britain's top stars (including Morecambe & Wise, The Two Ronnies, Max Bygraves, Ken Dodd and Stanley Baxter) and produced her own one-woman show based on the life of Adelina Patti.

Gillian is the founder, driving force and life-blood of the Concordia Foundation, focusing on "*building bridges through music and the arts*". Her extraordinary and tireless work with Concordia has taken her round the world from Windsor Castle to Vietnam and the South Bank to Cuba. Countless young professionals have had the benefit of her selfless determination and teaching; the ethic and purpose of the Foundation were endorsed by Mother Theresa and Gillian has since been awarded an O.B.E. for her achievements.

Mississippi Mud

Ingredients

2 eggs

1.5 cups sugar

.75 cup butter

.25 cup cocoa

.50 cup mixed nuts

1.5 cups flour

2 teaspoons vanilla, teaspoon salt

Small marshmallows

Method

Combine butter, sugar, eggs, cocoa and add flour and salt. Mix well. Add nuts and vanilla and pour into well-greased deep pan and bake for 30–35 minutes at 250C. Remove from the oven and cover with miniature marshmallows. Return to oven to melt.

Topping

.25 cup butter

.25 cup cocoa

4 oz. icing sugar

1 cup Carnation milk

1 teaspoon vanilla

.50 cup chopped nuts

Combine all ingredients and pour over the top of marshmallows. Let stand for at least two hours. Cut and serve in about 1 inch squares. Put into petit four cases. *Delicious!*

G&S in Bangkok with David Steadman and Richard Swerrun.

With Mother Theresa

Sir W. S. Gilbert

"You cannot eat breakfast all day,
Nor is it the act of a sinner,
When breakfast is taken away,
To turn his attention to dinner."

Trial by Jury

Vivian Tierney

Treacle Tart

Ingredients (Serves 4 to 6)

Shortcrust Pastry

175g (6oz) plain flour

75g (3oz) butter or margarine

1–2 tbs iced water

Method

Sift the flour into a bowl. Rub in the butter or margarine until the mixture resembles fine breadcrumbs. Add the water gradually and mix to a firm dough.

Turn out onto a floured surface and knead lightly. Roll out thinly to a 23cm (9inch) circle. Use to line an 18cm (7inch) flan ring placed on a baking sheet. Chill the flan and pastry trimmings for 15 minutes.

Filling

250g (8oz) golden syrup

75g (3oz) fresh white breadcrumbs

grated rind of ½ lemon

Mix the syrup, breadcrumbs and lemon rind together and spread over the pastry. Roll out the trimmings, cut into long narrow strips and make a lattice pattern over the filling.

Bake in a preheated moderately hot oven, 200°C (400°F), Gas Mark 6, for 30 to 35 minutes. Serve warm with cream.

Manchester Tart

Ingredients

25g sugar

25g desiccated coconut (or grated chocolate – optional)

100g margarine

1 jar jam

225g plain flour

1 banana (or 2, or 3 – depending on your taste)

30ml water and 230ml custard

For the pastry

1. Preheat oven to 190C (gas mark 5).
2. Mix flour and sugar, rub in fat.
3. Mix with cold water using a knife to cut and stir to form a dough.
4. Knead dough lightly on a floured surface.
5. Roll out and put in a flat tin.
6. Place a circle of greaseproof paper over the bottom of the tart and sprinkle a layer of rice or dried beans on top to prevent it rising (don't put it directly on the pastry).
7. Bake for 20 mins, remove the rice/beans and paper, return for 5 more minutes until crisp and golden.
8. Allow to cool.

For the filling

1. Make up custard according to instructions but missing out some liquid to make it thick, leave to cool slightly.
2. Dollop jam into the pastry case and spread around evenly.
3. Slice bananas and arrange on top of jam.
4. Pour partially cooled custard on top of the jam and bananas.
5. Sprinkle desiccated coconut on top of the custard if you like.
6. Leave to set in fridge. *Viv x*

149

Susan Jackson

Susan was Principal Soprano in the D'Oyly Carte from
1967–69 after seasons with the New Opera
Company and Glyndebourne. She had
previously completed her studies at the
Royal Northern College of Music and the
London Opera Centre, winning the
Leverhulme and Arts Council Scholarships.

Her G&S roles were Phyllis, Patience,
Josephine, Gianetta and Rose Maybud and she
would reprise Phyllis and Patience in 1987–88
at Gawsworth Hall, Cheshire. Susan also toured
in *A Waltz Dream* and appeared at the famous
Players' Theatre, London.

Bakewell Tart

Ingredients

Ready-made pastry
2 oz. butter
3 oz. sugar
2 eggs
3 oz. breadcrumbs
3 oz. almonds
Juice of lemon
Strawberry Jam

Method

For ease, buy ready-made pastry from the supermarket

Cream the butter, sugar and eggs

Add the breadcrumbs, almonds and lemon juice

Roll out the pastry case and place in a Pyrex dish

Line the case with strawberry jam

Pour the mixture into the case and put more jam on top

Bake in the oven at 180 degrees for an hour and ENJOY!!

As Always

Susie

Doreen Denny: Raspberry Jelly Cream

Brighton born Doreen Denny made her professional debut in grand opera – notably as Countess Ceprano in *Rigoletto* and Lola in *Cavalleria Rusticana*. From 1936 she spent four years with the D'Oyly Carte playing a mixture of soprano roles ranging from Fiametta in *The Gondoliers* to Elsie in *The Yeomen of the Guard*.

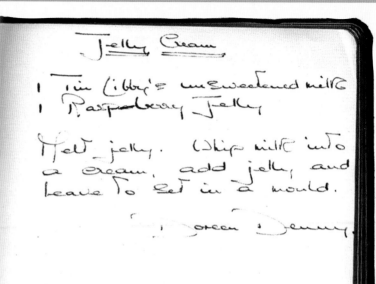

Jelly Cream

1 Tin Libby's unsweetened milk
1 Raspberry Jelly

Melt jelly. Whip milk into a cream, add jelly, and leave to set in a mould.

Doreen Denny.

Dorothy Chapman:
Trifle & Mock Poached Eggs

After operatic appearances at the Theatre Royal Drury Lane, Covent Garden and the Wigmore Hall, Dorothy joined the D'Oyly Carte in 1932 staying for three years.

Trifle.

Line a glass bowl with sponge fingers – moisten with fruit juice + table-spoonful of wine – add half pint of jelly. Leave to set. When set put a layer of fruit in season or tinned. + pour on a pint of custard. Before serving decorate with fruit + whipped cream + split almonds.

Mock Poached eggs.
Make one pint of vanilla blanc-mange. wet several small cups. + place a tinned apricot in each, cut side downwards. pour on blanc. mange. When set. turn out on dish + fill apricots with whipped cream.

Dorothy Chapman.

Joy Mornay: Special Trifle

Joy studied at the Guildhall School of Music and Drama and after appearances in pantomime and Vivian Ellis's *And So to Bed*, joined the D'Oyly Carte in 1954. Here she met her future husband Jon Ellison. In 1956, Joy left the Company and toured in *Chu Chin Chow* and *The Lilac Domino*, returning in 1959 as Guilia in *The Gondoliers*, Sacharissa in *Princess Ida* and Fleta in *Iolanthe*. She left again in 1965 but guested for the 1965–66 season at the Saville Theatre.

Love from
Joy

Ingredients
10 sponge fingers, broken up.
A little sherry, to taste
125g (4ozs) Any berries, such as strawberries, raspberries, blackberries etc.
I generally use blackberries, since we have climbing blackberries in the garden, lightly stewed and thickened with a little cornflower)
1 tub (250g) Mascarpone cheese.
140ml (5fl oz.) double cream
60g (2 oz.) sugar.
2 sliced bananas, 2 eggs

Method
Put the sponge fingers in a glass dish and pour sherry over, leaving to soak for a few minutes, then add the fruit.
Cream egg yolks with sugar, add Mascarpone cheese and beat until light.
Fold in stiffly beaten egg whites and spoon onto fruit mixture.
Whip cream until softly peaking, spread over trifle and scatter some flaked almonds and grated chocolate over the top.

Eleanor Evans (Fancourt): Snookie's Chocolate Blancmange

Born in 1893, Eleanor Evans trained at the Royal Academy of Music, where she first met her future husband Darrell Fancourt. She joined the D'Oyly Carte Chorus in 1921 and, in her early days, occasionally appeared as Lady Psyche, Plaintiff, Josephine and Gianetta. She was made Director of Productions in 1949 retiring from the Company in 1953. She died in 1969, aged 76.

Chocolate Blancmange.

1 Table spoonful of Cornflour.
1½ Table spoonful of Cadbury's Cocoa.
1½ "   "   " Sugar.
1 Pint of milk.

Mix cocoa & flour well with sugar. Mix in the milk, after boiling & bring the whole mixture to the boil. Put in a mould to cool. You will find this very good. I hope you have it often & your thoughts of me are as sweet as the mixture.

Snookie.

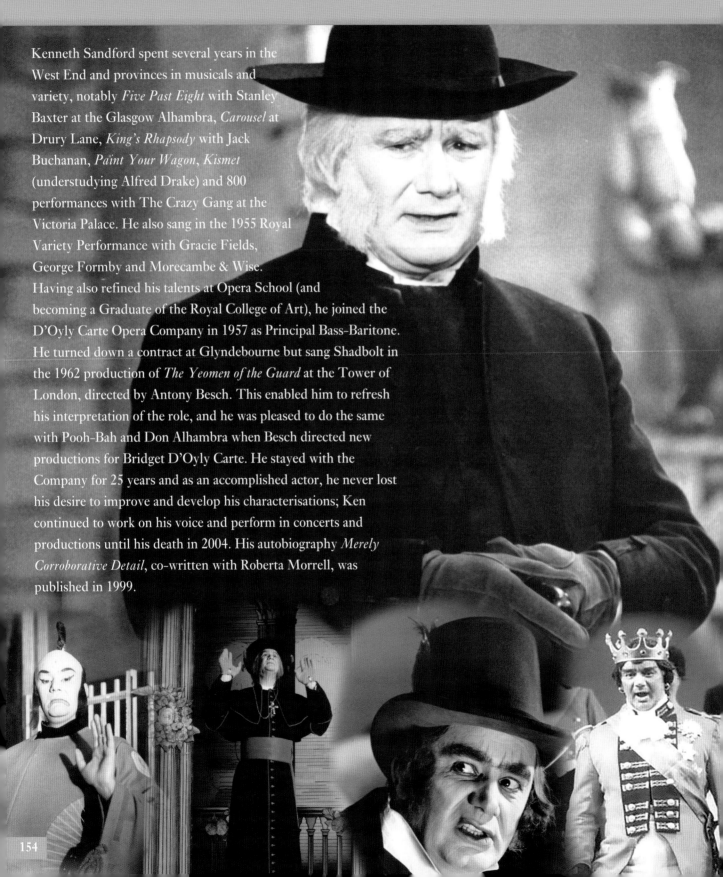

Kenneth Sandford

Kenneth Sandford spent several years in the West End and provinces in musicals and variety, notably *Five Past Eight* with Stanley Baxter at the Glasgow Alhambra, *Carousel* at Drury Lane, *King's Rhapsody* with Jack Buchanan, *Paint Your Wagon*, *Kismet* (understudying Alfred Drake) and 800 performances with The Crazy Gang at the Victoria Palace. He also sang in the 1955 Royal Variety Performance with Gracie Fields, George Formby and Morecambe & Wise. Having also refined his talents at Opera School (and becoming a Graduate of the Royal College of Art), he joined the D'Oyly Carte Opera Company in 1957 as Principal Bass-Baritone. He turned down a contract at Glyndebourne but sang Shadbolt in the 1962 production of *The Yeomen of the Guard* at the Tower of London, directed by Antony Besch. This enabled him to refresh his interpretation of the role, and he was pleased to do the same with Pooh-Bah and Don Alhambra when Besch directed new productions for Bridget D'Oyly Carte. He stayed with the Company for 25 years and as an accomplished actor, he never lost his desire to improve and develop his characterisations; Ken continued to work on his voice and perform in concerts and productions until his death in 2004. His autobiography *Merely Corroborative Detail*, co-written with Roberta Morrell, was published in 1999.

PEACH UPSIDE-DOWN PUDDING

Picnic with Anne Sessions and John Fryatt

Ingredients:

2 tbsps. golden syrup
½–¾ lb. peaches, sliced, or
an 11oz. can of sliced
peaches, drained
4 oz. butter
4 oz. caster sugar
2 eggs
½ level tsp. baking powder
6 oz. flour
Milk to mix

Grease well a 6-inch cake tin and put a round of greased paper at the bottom. Coat the base with golden syrup and arrange the peaches decoratively over this.

Cream the fat and sugar and beat in the eggs. Sift together the baking powder and flour and fold into the mixture, with a little milk to give a soft dropping consistency. Put the mixture into the tin, and bake in a fairly hot oven (400° F Mark 6) until well risen and brown - about 35 to 40 minutes. Turn the pudding out upside-down and serve with syrup sauce.

Upside-down Pudding can be varied by using other fruits - fresh, bottled or canned - or the sponge mixture can be flavoured with ginger, chocolate, lemon, or orange, coffee, etc. Serve with a suitably-flavoured sauce.

SYRUP SAUCE   4 tbsps. water
                     2 tbsps golden syrup
                     Juice of ½ a lemon
Mix all together and boil rapidly for a few minutes

Kennett Sandford

'somebody's birthday I suppose'

Bertha Lewis

Bertha Lewis first joined the D'Oyly Carte Company in 1906 aged 19 and played many of the smaller mezzo-soprano roles including Lady Saphir, Leila, Vittoria and Inez. She left in 1910 returning four years later as Principal Contralto; her success was immense and she is still regarded as one of the Company's brightest stars with a deep understanding of the characters and their place in the stories of the operas. Adored by her fans and revered by colleagues, she could be as formidable off-stage as she was when playing Gilbert's old ladies. Woebetide any errant chorister who got in her way in the wings or "upstart" conductor who messed around with her tempi (Malcolm Sargent). She was the stuff of which the theatre is made and her true "star" status was never more apparent than when she lay dying after a car crash in 1931; whilst her driver, Sir Henry Lytton, was slowly recovering, Bertha's injuries were far more serious; their story was closely followed on the BBC and in the press; H.M. Queen Mary, who much admired her work, made personal enquiries about her condition.

She died on Friday May 8th aged 44.

Her colleagues and friends were given the tragic news of her death after the performance of *Iolanthe* that same night.

Raspberry Pudding

Raspberry Pudding.

Weight of 2 eggs in butter & flour
"   " 1 "   in sugar.
teaspoonful carbonate of soda.
2 tablespoonfuls jam.
Beat butter & sugar to a cream
add eggs beaten. add flour carb.
soda then jam. Boil 2 hours
serve with sauce.

Bertha Lewis.

Gwladys Gowrie: Summer Pudding

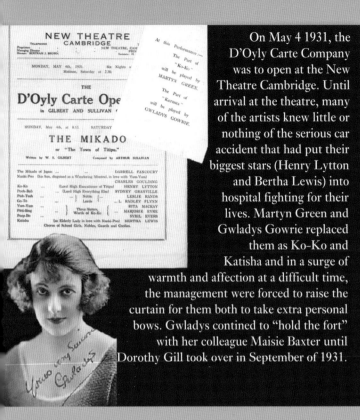

On May 4 1931, the D'Oyly Carte Company was to open at the New Theatre Cambridge. Until arrival at the theatre, many of the artists knew little or nothing of the serious car accident that had put their biggest stars (Henry Lytton and Bertha Lewis) into hospital fighting for their lives. Martyn Green and Gwladys Gowrie replaced them as Ko-Ko and Katisha and in a surge of warmth and affection at a difficult time, the management were forced to raise the curtain for them both to take extra personal bows. Gwladys continued to "hold the fort" with her colleague Maisie Baxter until Dorothy Gill took over in September of 1931.

Summer Pudding

Line a basin with thinly cut bread and fill with stewed fruit of any kind. When the basin is full, cover the top with bread and cover until the whole is set. (Place a weight on top while it is standing) When cold, turn out in glass dish and serve with whipped cream.

Gwladys Gowrie

Only one pudding to be eaten at one meal!

Marjorie Wyeth: Oven Baked Rice Pudding

Marjorie Wyeth was a contralto chorister with D'Oyly Carte from 1931–36 and for a six week season at the Hippodrome Golders Green in 1940.

Rice Pudding (In them!)

A quart of milk.
Small teacup of Rice (unpolished)
Two tablespoons of Sugar
Grated nutmeg.
Wash the rice. put in a pie dish with other ingredients & bake for one hour.

Marjorie.

Billy's Christmas Pudd

C. William Morgan was born in Monmouth and served the D'Oyly Carte management for thirty years as a chorister, understudy, purveyor of small roles and finally as Assistant Stage Manager. He had substituted for both Martyn Green and Grahame Clifford on occasion and played Major Murgatroyd in *Patience* for most of his time with the Company. He left in 1950, became a popular director ("producer") for amateur companies and died in Worcester in 1974.

A Christmas Pudding.

1 lb Beef Suet (finely chopped)
1 lb Bread Crumbs. (Stale bread)
1 lb Castor Sugar
2 lb Valencia Raisins
1 lb Sultanes
1 lb Currants
6 ozs Mixed Peel.
½ oz ground ~~Almonds~~ Nutmeg.
½ oz ,, Cinnamon
Small Salt Spoon of ground Clove.
Grated Rind & Juice of two Lemons.
½ lb best apples. (Bramley Seedlings) to weigh ½ lb without the peel.
6 fresh Eggs.
Breakfast cup of Self Raising Flour.
Good Pinch of Salt.
2 wine glasses of Rum or Brandy.

Stone & Chop Raisins in halves. Mix bread crumbs, Suet, Flour, Salt, Cinnamon, Nutmeg, Clove & Sugar. Then add fruit & mix well. Beat up the eggs & add the rum. Pour this into the other mixture & stir in till all thoroughly mixed. Lastly chop the apples & add to the pudding just before putting into the basins. Steam for 12 hours at least.

Billy Morgan.

Anna Vincent: Mincemeat Parcels

Anna was a member of the D'Oyly Carte Chorus from 1964-67 and regularly sang Fiametta in *The Gondoliers*.

MINCEMEAT PARCELS

1 packet filo pastry, defrosted
411g (14.5oz) jar mincemeat
grated rind of 1 orange
15g (½oz) butter, melted
1 tablespoon icing sugar
Cooking Time 10-15 minutes
Makes 8

1. Trim the pastry sheets and cut into 24 squares approximately 15cm (6 inch).

2. Place 3 filo pastry squares on top of each other at a slight angle to form a 12 pointed "star".

3. Place a heaped tablespoon of the mincemeat in the centre and add a little grated orange rind. Carefully pick up the pastry corners to enclose the filling and press together to form a "parcel".

4. Repeat with the remaining pastry and mincemeat to make 8 "parcels". Arrange on a baking tray and lightly brush the parcels with melted butter.

5. Place in a preheated oven 190°C, 375°F, Gas mark 5 for 10-15 minutes until crisp and golden.

6. Dust with icing sugar. Serve hot or cold.

159

Leonard Osborn

As his many fans will testify, Leonard Osborn was one of the D'Oyly Carte matinée idols. He had first sung in the chorus from 1937–40 prior to service in the Royal Air Force for the rest of the war. On his return in 1946, he was made Principal Tenor and is still rated as the definitive Richard Dauntless in *Ruddigore* (his favourite role). He had natural charisma, good looks and a commanding stage presence; the press often commented on his characterization and beautifully enunciated portrayals. He often struggled with medically-based vocal problems which led to his departure from the Company in 1959. He became Stage Director for the D'Oyly Carte in 1977 – a season which included the Royal Command Performance of *H.M.S. Pinafore* at Windsor Castle. He left in 1980 and died on 28 September 1994 aged 79.

"Hollywood could not wish for a more winsome heart-throb"
Bristol Evening Post

Spotted Dick Dauntless

Ingredients

125g suet
250g self-raising flour
80g caster sugar
180g currants

Grated zest of one lemon
and one orange
150ml milk (Full Fat)
Pinch of salt

Method

Place the flour, salt, currants, sugar, suet and zest into a bowl.

Add 150ml of the milk and mix to a dough. Keep the dough moist and add more of the milk if needs be.

Shape into a roll and place on baking parchment.

Wrap loosely and tie ends.

Cover and steam over a saucepan of boiling water for about an hour and a half. Occasionally top up the water as needed.

Serve with custard.

Leonard as Florian in *Princess Ida*. The marionette was made for him by one of his numerous female admirers and is shown here on display at Oak Hall, Sussex as part of the Melvyn Tarran Collection

Leonard Osborn

Richard Walker

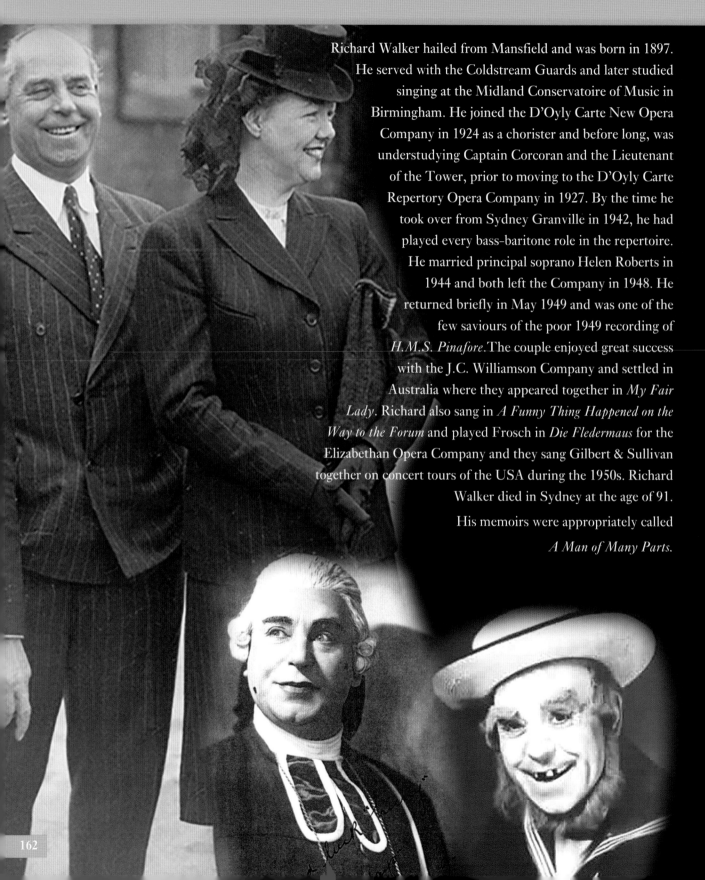

Richard Walker hailed from Mansfield and was born in 1897. He served with the Coldstream Guards and later studied singing at the Midland Conservatoire of Music in Birmingham. He joined the D'Oyly Carte New Opera Company in 1924 as a chorister and before long, was understudying Captain Corcoran and the Lieutenant of the Tower, prior to moving to the D'Oyly Carte Repertory Opera Company in 1927. By the time he took over from Sydney Granville in 1942, he had played every bass-baritone role in the repertoire. He married principal soprano Helen Roberts in 1944 and both left the Company in 1948. He returned briefly in May 1949 and was one of the few saviours of the poor 1949 recording of *H.M.S. Pinafore.* The couple enjoyed great success with the J.C. Williamson Company and settled in Australia where they appeared together in *My Fair Lady*. Richard also sang in *A Funny Thing Happened on the Way to the Forum* and played Frosch in *Die Fledermaus* for the Elizabethan Opera Company and they sang Gilbert & Sullivan together on concert tours of the USA during the 1950s. Richard Walker died in Sydney at the age of 91.

His memoirs were appropriately called *A Man of Many Parts.*

Make some pancakes in the usual way,
but very thin, and spread each with
some thick purée of pears flavoured
with vanilla. Fold each pancake in four
and arrange them all on a dish,
sprinkle them with sugar and glaze
them quickly with a salamander, or
under the gas-grill. Then pour over
some curaçao, and set it alight as
you bring the dish to the table.

R. Walker.

12-2-34.

Joyce Wright

Joyce was born in Leicester and raised in Glasgow. After appearances in music festivals and as a professional pianist in a dance orchestra, she joined the D'Oyly Carte Opera Company in 1947 as a chorister; she was immediately given minor roles (Leila & Peep-Bo) and in 1951 became a Principal, her name becoming synonomous with the roles of Cousin Hebe, Pitti-Sing, Iolanthe, Mad Margaret, Lady Angela, Tessa, Phoebe and Edith. She sang in several BBC broadcasts with the Company and was featured on the cover of the *Radio Times* during the 1961 season at the Savoy. Joyce left the D'Oyly Carte in 1962 and played Phoebe in *The Yeomen of the Guard* at the Tower of London in the same year. She also did further work with the BBC and was much in demand as a Director of amateur societies. There was great happiness when she appeared as a special guest at the D'Oyly Carte Reunion Concert *Together Again* at Manchester Free Trade Hall in 1993.

Fruit Pavlova

At the site of the old Bijou Theatre, Paignton with Philip Potter, Gillian Knight (r) and Jennifer Toye

Joyce with husband Cyril

PAVLOVA

4 Egg Whites	½ Pint Double Cream
8 oz Caster Sugar	¼ Pint Single Cream
1 teaspoon Vanilla Essence	Fruit of your choice – sliced strawberries, pineapple, raspberries – or whatever
1 teaspoon Vinegar	
2 level teaspoons Cornflour	

Whisk egg whites stiffly. Continue whisking and gradually add the sugar until very stiff. Beat in the vanilla, vinegar and cornflour. Spread the mixture in a circle on <u>non-stick</u> paper on a baking sheet.

Bake just below the centre of the oven for about one hour at Gas 1-2 or 140°/150°C. Remove from oven when meringue shows 'cracking'. <u>Leave to cool</u>. Turn upside down onto a flat serving plate and gently remove the paper.

TO SERVE: Whip creams together until they just hold their shape. Pile layers of cream and fruit –OR– decorate with fruit on top – as you wish.

*God bless
& much love.
Joyce*

165

Winnie Melville &
Derek Oldham

Winnie Melville had a flourishing career in musical comedy and revue with appearances in the West End and at the Folies-Bergères. London shows included *See-Saw* and *Whirled into Happiness* where she met her future husband Derek Oldham. In 1926–27, she was leading lady in *The Student Prince*, *Princess Charming* and *The Vagabond King* joining the D'Oyly Carte Opera Company as Principal Soprano in 1929 for one season. She continued to tour but died prematurely in 1937 at the age of 42.

Born in Accrington in 1887, Derek Oldham remains one of the most famous D'Oyly Carte artistes. However, he was also a major star in the West End; after his debut at the London Pavilion and a successful run in *The Chocolate Soldier*, he joined the East Lancashire Regiment and was awarded the Military Cross for gallantry in Macedonia in 1918. He undertook the first of his D'Oyly Carte contracts from 1919–22, joining them for the landmark season at the Princes Theatre. After his debut as Marco in *The Gondoliers* he was challenged by J.M. Gordon, the formidable stage director, who, despite Derek enthusing about the "*lovely time*" he'd had, damned his performance as being "*thoroughly common!!*" (This, in Derek's own words!)

He then returned to a glittering life in musical comedy including *Madam Pompadour*, *Rose Marie*, *The Merry Widow* and The Vagabond King. Whilst in Whirled into Happiness at the Lyric, he met his future wife Winnie Melville. He returned to the D'Oyly Carte for the 1929–30 season and again for the prestigious American Tour of 1934–35. He was, by now, a star name and on the return visit to the USA in 1936, it was stipulated by the promoters that Derek Oldham was again part of the Company. During this tour, he also sang at the White House for President Roosevelt's inauguration party. His career continued in London until 1958 (*Verdict*, Strand Theatre) and he subsequently retired to Hayling Island. Derek Oldham died in 1968.

Fraises à la Melville

It was while holidaying in Paris that a French *maître d'hôtel* handed me a menu at *déjeuner* one day with Fraises à la Melville taking the place of a sweet. When I had tried them, he said, "If mademoiselle wants to make them at home, she should just hull a pound of strawberries, put them in a glass dish, sprinkle lightly with maraschino and 1 teaspoon sherry, and allow dish to stand on ice for half an hour before serving with crème fouettée – simply cream whipped over ice, sweetened with caster sugar, and flavoured to taste with vanilla or a liqueur."

Our good wishes
Winnie Melville
& Derek Oldham

The Menu Card for Richard D'Oyly Carte's 1887 river trip to Cliveden via D'Oyly Carte Island.
The entire Savoy Company was transported in three steam boats.

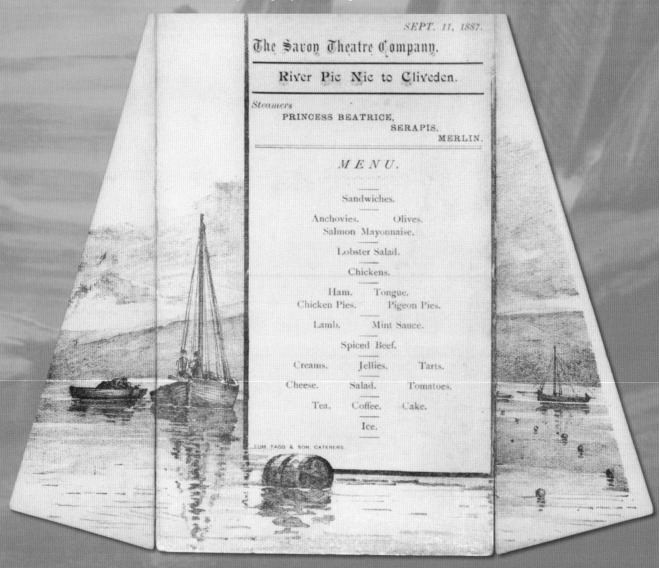

SEPT. 11, 1887.

The Savoy Theatre Company.

River Pic Nic to Cliveden.

Steamers
PRINCESS BEATRICE,
SERAPIS,
MERLIN.

MENU.

Sandwiches.

Anchovies.   Olives.
Salmon Mayonnaise.

Lobster Salad.

Chickens.

Ham.   Tongue.
Chicken Pies.   Pigeon Pies.

Lamb.   Mint Sauce.

Spiced Beef.

Creams.   Jellies.   Tarts.

Cheese.   Salad.   Tomatoes.

Tea.   Coffee.   Cake.

Ice.

TOM TAGG & SON, CATERERS.

D'Oyly Carte Island,
Weybridge

"Sighing softly to the river,
Comes the loving breeze;
Setting nature all a-quiver,
Rustling through the trees"

Major General Stanley
The Pirates of Penzance

Dame Bridget
D'Oyly Carte

Lyndsie
Holland

Cynthia Morey

C
A
K
E
S

Treats
&
Picnics

169

John Reed O.B.E.

John was the much loved patter man of the D'Oyly Carte for 20 years following eight years understudying Peter Pratt. Adorable in *The Mikado*, heart-wrenching in *The Yeomen of the Guard*, he managed to find the inner soul of his characters and connect with the audience like no other. His natural warmth and humour meant he never relied on tricks, vulgarity or over-playing.

"His nimble dancing, characterful light-baritone singing, and the business he was able to introduce into encores and elsewhere within the generally rigid D'Oyly Carte constraints, soon helped to establish his own loyal following, and the personal rapport he enjoyed with his fans grew to legendary status" (**Andrew Lamb**)

Like Kenneth Sandford, he revelled in the opportunity to re-work his characters, not least in the Antony Besch production of *The Gondoliers*, and was a joy to behold in the 1971 Sorcerer and the Centenary *Utopia Ltd*. He was, however, never keen on playing King Gama in *Princess Ida* or Major General Stanley in *The Pirates of Penzance*. In the latter role, his first ever performance when standing in for Peter Pratt was stressful to say the least. According to Beryl Dixon, *"we didn't know which verse was coming next. At one point John turned upstage and cried 'EEELLLLPPP' in total panic!!!"*

Throughout his career, he always found time to work with and help new artists and to change or modify his own performance. Although he chose to leave the D'Oyly Carte in 1979 he was a surprise Guest Artist at the Theatre Royal Nottingham and for the final season of the old Company at the Adelphi in London. He continued to work in the USA for many years to come especially in New York, Boulder, Dallas and with the Washington Opera in *La Belle Helene* and *M Choufleuri*. In 2006, his autobiography *Nothing Whatever to Grumble At* was published; John died on his 94th birthday in 2010.

"He was, quite simply, a phenomenon."
The Times

Sponge Cake

with home-made Lemon Curd filling

Lemon Curd Ingredients

3oz. Butter
8oz. Caster Sugar
3 eggs
2 lemons

Method

Melt butter in a 2½ pint size bowl for
1½ minutes.
Finely grate the lemon rind.
Beat sugar, eggs, lemon rind and juice
into
melted butter – mixing well.
Cook in a microwave oven, set at high
for about 3 mins, until mixture coats
back of a spoon and then stir very briskly
as mixture thickens.
Pour into warm jars, cover and seal.
Mixture will store for two weeks.

Sponge Cake Ingredients

6oz. Margarine
6oz. Sugar
6oz. S.R. Flour
3 eggs

Method

Beat all the ingredients well, in a bowl, or electric
mixer.
Line an 8" tin and put in the mixture.
Place in pre-heated oven and cook at 180 degrees C
for 30-35mins.
Test with a skewer.
When the sponge is cold, slice in half and fill with
the lemon curd. Dust the top with icing or caster
sugar and serve with a nice cup of tea.

John Reed.

Sibylle Thomas: Sponge Mixture

Sibylle was a chorister with the Company from 1923–28, 1929–34 and finally from 1940–46.

She was married to Jerome Stephens who was Stage Manager from 1949-61.

Spone mixture

The weight of two eggs in Butter, castor sugar, self raising flour. mise the sugar with softened butter and add flour & eggs Bake in two tins for about 20 minutes.

Tibby

Gladys Bone:

Orange Sponge

Gladys made her debut in the D'Oyly Carte Chorus at Brighton in 1929; she remained with the Company until 1938.

Orange Sponge.

Juice of an orange.
3 eggs.
1 breakfast-cupful of self-raising flour.
¾ breakfast-cupful of castor sugar.

Separate the yolks and whites of eggs and beat the whites to a stiff froth for about 15 minutes. Add the beaten yolks of the eggs and then the juice of the orange. Also though a sieve and then the flour - also though a sieve and mix well.

P.T.O

Separate the mixture into two even tins and bake in a warm oven for 18 minutes. cool on a rack and when quite cold, make it into a sandwich with whipped cream.

Gladys. (Bone)

Josephine Curtis:
Victoria Sandwich

Australian Josephine Curtis was a member of the D'Oyly Carte Chorus from 1933–36 and understudied the Principal Contralto roles played by Dorothy Gill and Evelyn Gardiner. As was the norm, she played Inez in *The Gondoliers* but also sang Katisha on the 1936 recording of *The Mikado*, even though the popular Dorothy Gill was still in the Company.

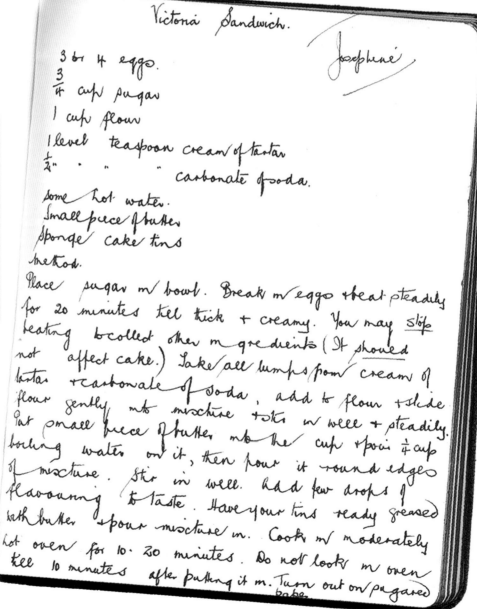

Victoria Sandwich.

Josephine

3 or 4 eggs.
$\frac{3}{4}$ cup sugar
1 cup flour
1 level teaspoon cream of tartar
$\frac{1}{2}$" " " carbonate of soda.
Some hot water.
Small piece of butter
Sponge cake tins
Method.
Place sugar in bowl. Break in eggs + beat steadily for 20 minutes till thick + creamy. You may stop beating to collect other ingredients (It should not affect cake.) Take all lumps from cream of tartar + carbonate of soda, add to flour + slide flour gently into mixture + stir in well + steadily. Put small piece of butter into the cup + pour $\frac{3}{4}$ cup boiling water on it, then pour it round edges of mixture. Stir in well. Add few drops of flavouring to taste. Have your tins ready greased with butter + pour mixture in. Cook in moderately hot oven for 10. 20 minutes. Do not look in oven till 10 minutes after putting it in. Turn out on papered paper.

Ann Drummond-Grant

A much-loved and respected artist who after a short spell in the chorus became D'Oyly Carte's Principal Soprano in 1937. Having promoted her, the management then decided she was too tall and "Drummie" left the Company for a career in Musical Comedy, Operetta, Pantomime and Summer seasons. She married Isidore Godfrey in 1940 and was a guest mezzo-soprano on the early Decca recordings. In 1951, she replaced Ella Halman as Principal Contralto, playing the roles with great and popular success until May 1959.

On the 1955 tour of America, one of the dressers in New York, a trained nurse, confided in Beryl Dixon her concerns that "Miss Grant might be unwell"; for another four years her vibrant stage performances and memorable recordings of Katisha, Ruth and the Duchess of Plaza-Toro (live from the Prince's Theatre) were to disguise the fact that she was suffering from the cancer that would eventually claim her life on 11 September 1959.

"... she was far too good for us!"
Brenda Bennett

"One of the very few people who have sung the contralto parts, not as hard, beastly women, but with true understanding of their light and shade."
Darrell Fancourt

174

Ann (left) at a reception with D'Oyly Carte colleagues
including Neville Griffiths and Jean Hindmarsh

Beach picnic with husband
Isidore Godfrey and Cynthia Morey

Oven Scones.

2 breakfastcupfuls plain flour.
½ teaspoonful baking soda
½   "   cream of tartar.
½   "   salt.
Piece of butter size of an egg.
Sufficient milk to mix.

Sift flour into basin, add soda,
cream of tartar & salt. Rub butter
into flour etc, mix all well
together, add sufficient milk to
make nice soft consistency. Bake
in moderate oven till nicely
fired.

Drummie.

Mary Sansom

Originally from Taunton, Mary studied singing in Bristol and successfully auditioned for the D'Oyly Carte in 1956 as a chorister and understudy, also playing Celia in *Iolanthe* and Zorah in *Ruddigore*. She became a Principal Soprano in 1959 and her repertoire included what were to be regarded as her signature roles – Phyllis and Patience. She also enjoyed success as Gianetta, Rose Maybud and Yum-Yum – roles she always played with great charm; she and her husband, Alan Barrett, also played opposite one other as the Plaintiff and Learned Judge in *Trial by Jury*. From 1964, she focused on raising their children also finding time to direct amateur societies. For 25 years, she helped run the family costuming business Barrett's of Bath and made occasional appearances on television. Mary died in April 2010.

Mary's Carrot Cake

8 oz	Soft Butter
8 oz	Brown Sugar
3	Eggs
8 oz	Plain White Flour
2 Tspns	Ground Cinnamon
2 Tspns	Baking Powder
10 oz	Grated Carrot
2½ oz	Chopped Walnuts
1½ oz	Raisins

Topping

8 oz	Cream Cheese
2 Tspns	Water
2 oz	Icing Sugar
2 Tspns	Lemon Juice
	Grated Lemon Rind

Cutting the "Ruddigore 75th Anniversary cake at the Savoy with John Reed

Method

Cream the butter and sugar and add the beaten eggs little by little. Sift together the flour, baking powder, and spice and fold into creamed mixture. Add the carrots nuts and raisins
Bake in an 8 inch tin for about an hour at regulo 4 or 175°C

Mary Sansom

Mary (centre) backstage with Peggy Ann Jones (left) and Joyce Wright

Cynthia Morey

The multi-talented bundle of energy and joy that is Cynthia Morey trained at the Royal College of Music and joined the D'Oyly Carte Opera Company in 1951. After a short time in the chorus and playing small parts, she became a Principal Soprano playing Yum-Yum, Phyllis, Rose Maybud, Gianetta and the title role in the new 1957 production of *Patience*. She left the Company later that year to join Sadler's Wells Opera and appears on their recordings of *Iolanthe* and *La Vie Parisienne*; she also toured in their productions of *Orpheus in the Underworld* and *The Merry Widow* in Australia and New Zealand. In the West End she appeared in *Robert and Elizabeth*, *Fiddler on the Roof*, *Gone With the Wind*, *Me and My Girl*, *Can-Can* and *Anything Goes*. Other engagements have included *My Fair Lady* in Canada, and the film *Quartet* with Dustin Hoffman. She is a talented artist and illustrator, a writer (*Inclined to Dance and Sing* and *A Set of Curious Chances*) and was collaborator on John Reed's autobiography.

With her friend, the late John Fryatt, she wrote the brilliant pantomime *The Sleeping Beauty of Savoy*.

Infallible Fruit Cake

INFALLIBLE FRUIT CAKE- (no *Patience* required!)

I'm not sure where this recipe came from originally- some of you may know it already, but many friends who encounter it for the first time say, 'What a lovely moist cake- I can never make a fruit cake like this!' and I feel rather a cheat, because it is *so* easy. In fact, I have occasionally made the recipe with 1½ times the quantity of ingredients, covered it with almond paste and icing, and used it as a Christmas cake. And you can make it at the last minute! Here it is- (I've used imperial measures- metric equivalents seemed unsuitable for a G & S cookery book!)

12oz mixed dried fruit
¼ lb margarine
1 cup water
1 cup sugar- (I use half caster, half soft brown)
1 teaspoon bicarbonate of soda

Put all ingredients in a saucepan, bring to the boil and simmer for five minutes. When cool, add two cups self-raising flour and one egg. Mix well, place in greased and lined tin, and bake in moderate oven (Gas mark 4) for approximately 50 minutes. Allow to cool slightly before turning out of tin.

With much love
Cynthia

Cynthia (right) with John Fryatt, Patience Pratt and Melvyn Tarran. Patience is the widow of Peter Pratt and daughter of Leo Sheffield.

"We are dainty little fairies,
ever singing, ever dancing"

Cynthia's Iolanthe Fairy Cakes

FAIRY CAKES

6 oz butter
6 oz caster sugar   3 eggs
6 oz self-raising flour
2 oz ground rice
A little milk to mix
Icing sugar   Glacé cherries
Vanilla essence
Gas mark 7   425°

Cream butter and sugar, beat in eggs.
Mix dry ingredients and add to the mixture,
together with a little milk and a few drops of vanilla essence.
Half fill paper cake cases and bake for about 15 minutes.
When cold, sprinkle with icing sugar
and put a cherry on top of each cake.

Royston Nash

Until his retirement in 2007, Royston enjoyed a long and distinguished career in music.

After studying at the Royal Marines School and the Royal Academy, with mentoring by Rudolfe Kempe and Sir Malcolm Sargent, Royston was appointed Bandmaster with the Royal Marines and subsequently would serve as Director of Music to the Commander-in-Chief, Mediterranean, Portsmouth and at the Royal Marines School in Deal. He made his first appearance with the D'Oyly Carte Opera Company in 1970, when, as Captain Nash, he conducted the Royal Marines Band in a guest appearance on the last night of the Sadler's Wells season. Later that year he joined the Company and became Musical Director in March 1971 with the new production of *The Sorcerer*. His tenure included the memorable Centenary Season at the Savoy, a Royal Command Performance at Windsor Castle and several significant recordings with the Royal Philharmonic Orchestra.

In 1979, Royston moved to the United States to become Music Director of the Nashua Symphony and the Cape Cod Symphony; such was his huge success at Cape Cod that he was made Musical Director Laureate for life.

He was founder of Symphony By The Sea, has been Music Director of the Cape Ann Symphony and a professor at Boston Conservatory of Music. Royston died on 4 April 2016

Caramel Layer Cake

Reunited with John Reed at the
Cape Cod Symphony

Have ready your favourite 2–layer yellow cake or
sponge cake.

Put 2 tins of condensed milk into a saucepan. The tins
are to remain sealed. They will not explode. Cover the
tins completely with water and top-up when required.
Cover the pan and boil for 3½ hours. After 3½ hours
remove tins and cool. The process of boiling the tins
will turn the sweetened condensed milk into caramel.
When the tins are cool, open them. Spread the contents
of one tin on first layer. Top with the second layer and
spread contents of second tin on top and sides of cake.

Very simple and easy.

Nancy Ray & Charles Leslie

Nancy was the longest serving member of the female chorus in the history of the Company – 28 years from 1910 to 1938. During this time she played most of the smaller soprano roles including Fleta, Lady Ella, Sacharissa, Fiametta and Zorah in *Ruddigore*. Husband Charles spent a mere 21 years of his life with D'Oyly Carte and in his early seasons, understudied Mountararat in *Iolanthe* and Arac in *Princess Ida*; he regularly played the smaller roles of Giorgio, Scynthius and 1st Citizen in *The Yeomen of the Guard* until around 1928.

The D'Oyly Carte Opera Company posing at Niagara Falls

Delicious Cake   No cooking

Cream together. 1/4 lb. Fresh Butter.
1/4 lb. Castor Sugar. 1/4 Grated Almonds.
then ~~Half~~ Wineglass of Whisky

Line 5" padding basin with 1/2 lb
sponge fingers sugar side to the basin
break fingers for bottom of basin
fill with the creamed mixture, and
cover with some of the remainder of
sponge fingers.

Cover with a plate with
a heavy weight on Top. and
leave to mature for 3 days. and
turn out on a cake plate.

Nancy & Leslie

Ceinwen Jones

Lovely Cei was born 16 September 1912, adored music and appreciated good singers, especially from her native Wales. She was in the D'Oyly Carte Opera Company from July 1946 till August 1963 as a chorister, also playing Vittoria in *The Gondoliers* (which she recorded) and an occasional Inez, Kate (*Pirates*) and Leila; she politely declined a request from Bridget D'Oyly Carte to audition for the Principal Contralto understudy job. Ceinwen married Bert Newby (chorister and, later on, Company Manager) in New York in 1955 and lived in their charming apartment in Hampstead Garden Suburb until shortly before her death.

Welsh Cakes

Light refreshments in America with Cis Blain
(Wardrobe Mistress) and Christene Palmer, 1966

With Ella Halman, 1980's

Ingredients

8oz. flour
4–5oz. margarine
1 egg
2oz. Caster sugar
2oz. Currants
Lard to grease the pan

Method

Rub the margarine into the flour.

Add the sugar and mix.

Whisk the egg and add to the mixture; add enough water to make a sticky dough.

Roll out onto a floured board.

Cut into 2-3 inch circles.

Grease the pan with lard. Heat (medium).

Drop in the prepared circles.

Turn frequently until golden; drop the heat as neccesary to prevent over-cooking.

Remove from the pan and sprinkle with either sugar or butter.

Ceinwen's Tip:
"A heavy pan is preferable as these cakes were originally baked on a griddle. However, an ordinary pan will serve the purpose."

Love
Ceinwen

Leo Sheffield

Born in 1873, he joined D'Oyly Carte in 1906 under the direction of W.S. Gilbert. In 1909, he appeared in *Fallen Faires*, *The Chocolate Soldier* and *Twelfth Night* before rejoining D'Oyly Carte as Principal Baritone from 1915 to 1928, returning one last time for the Savoy Season 1929–30. He was immensely popular and highly rated by Gilbert. He continued his success in London and on tour starring with Rex Harrison, Stanley Holloway and Anna Neagle. He also sang for ENSA, and in revivals of *The Chocolate Soldier*, *The Beggar's Opera*, *The Gypsy Baron* and *Naughty Marietta* (alongside Derek Oldham). Leo was also featured in the BBC radio story of Gilbert and Sullivan. He died in 1951.

Sheffield Parkin

Ingredients

4ozs (110g) butter

4ozs sugar

2ozs (55g) black treacle

7ozs (200g) syrup (golden syrup)

8ozs oatmeal (medium)

4ozs flour (self-raising)

2 tsp (ground) ginger

2 eggs (medium) beaten

Salt (pinch)

Method

Over a moderate heat, melt together the butter, sugar, treacle and syrup. Don't over heat!

Allow to cool a little.

Sprinkle the oatmeal, flour, ginger and spice into a mixture. Create a well in the middle of the bowl, add the melted butter and 'fold'.

Add the eggs and milk and mix together.

Pour into an oven tin (baking tin, greased and lined).

Bake for a good hour and 30 minutes in a moderate heated oven** but keep watch!!

When done, allow to stand for about 20 minutes; remove from the tin and let the Parkin cool down.

"Do so at the start of the week and keep in a tin. Enjoy on Saturday after the matinee."

**Pre-heated 140C, 120C fan; Gas Mark 1

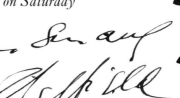

Margaret Dobson

Margaret was a member of the D'Oyly Carte from 1952-56; she had sung from the age of 3 and after training at the Royal College of Music toured in Emile Littler's production of *Lilac Time*. Her time in the Company was spent as a chorister and understudy also playing most of the smaller soprano roles including Lady Ella, Kate (*Yeomen*), Fleta and Celia in *Iolanthe*, Isabel, First Bridesmaid and Plaintiff in *Trial by Jury*, Guilia and Ruth in *Ruddigore*. She later continued to sing in oratorio and concerts; after raising her family, she spent over twenty years teaching music.

To Melvyn in Memory of a wonderful day.
Maggie Dobson

Granny's Gingerbread

INGREDIENTS:

3 CUPS PLAIN FLOUR (SIFTED)

1½ CUPS CASTER SUGAR

½ lb. MARGARINE

2 dessertspoons BLACK TREACLE

2 " " GOLDEN SYRUP

2 CUPS HOT WATER

2 heaped teaspoons BICARBONATE OF SODA

2 " " GINGER (I use 4!!)

PINCH OF SALT

METHOD: (TIN SIZE APPROX. 9"×11")

1. MIX FLOUR, SUGAR, SALT, GINGER IN LARGE BOWL

2. MELT MARGARINE & SYRUP IN PAN. POUR INTO MIDDLE OF DRY INGREDIENTS.

3. STIR ONE SPOONFUL OF BICARB. INTO ONE CUP OF HOT WATER, ADD TO MIXTURE AND STIR

4. REPEAT WITH SECOND CUP OF HOT WATER AND BICARB.

5. STIR ALL WELL AND POUR INTO GREASED ROASTING TIN. (COVER TIN BOTTOM WITH GREASEPROOF PAPER)

6. BAKE IN MODERATE (GAS 4) OVEN FOR ONE HOUR. COOL IN TIN. CUT INTO SQUARES.

" Whenever I bake this, the rich aroma takes me back to childhood days when my two brothers and I used to spend our summer vacations with our grandparents.

They lived in a Cumbrian village where my grandfather was a miner. The village was surrounded by fells and the main meandering street was a cobbled one which made a great percussion instrument in response to the footwear of the day- clogs!

My grandmother was a very strong woman in spite of (or perhaps because of) having lived a hard life – a miner's wife who had brought up her own two daughters plus three orphaned nephews, and had also worked in a munitions factory during the 1914-18 war."

Most Sincere Wishes

Margaret Dobson

Catherine Ferguson

Catherine Ferguson's early stage appearances included *The Cinema Star* and *The Girl in the Taxi* giving her the opportunity to develop her stage craft prior to joining the D'Oyly Carte Repertory Opera Company in 1918 as Principal Soubrette. Except for the 1919 Princes Theatre season, when she was moved to smaller roles to facilitate the return of Nellie Briercliffe, she played Constance, Melissa et al until she retired from the Company in 1923; she had married her colleague Arthur Lucas in 1920 but increasing deafness had made it impossible for her to continue on the stage. She died in 1972.

Walnut Cream Toffee

Walnut Cream Toffee

Put 1lb. granulated sugar,

$^1/_2$ pint thin cream, and

1 tablespoon golden syrup into an enamelled pan.

Stir well until it comes to a boil;

after which boil from 15 to 20 minutes,

then remove from saucepan, stir in 4ozs. shelled and

chopped walnuts, and $^1/_2$ teaspoon essence of vanilla.

Now place pan in a basin of cold water,

and stir quickly until toffee becomes thick,

pour into a buttered tin, mark in squares with a knife,

then leave till hard and cold.

It can then be easily broken into squares.

Catherine Feepooch

"*We are all fond of toffee … and toffee in moderation is a capital thing.*"

Colonel Calverley & Lieut. The Duke of Dunstable: *Patience*

Alan Barrett

Alan sang with the opera company from 1956–63 and was often seen as Major Murgatroyd in *Patience*, Samuel in *The Pirates of Penzance* and the Associate in *Trial by Jury*.

Alan and the Baddeley Cake

The legacy of Robert Baddeley 1733-94; cook, actor.

"*The sum of One hundred pounds Stock in the three per cent Consolidated Bank Annuities may be purchased immediately after my decease . . . to produce as nearly as possible the Annual Sum of Three Pounds which . . . I direct shall be applied and expended in the purchase of a twelfth Cake or Cakes and Wine or Punch or both of them which . . . it is my request that the Ladies and Gentlemen performers of Drury Lane Theatre . . . will do me the favor to accept on twelfth night in every year in the Green Room . . .*"

From 1975-2010 the Baddeley Cake was made by Alan. Unlike his predecessors, Alan always used the resident production at Drury lane as the theme of the cake, varying the design each year in the event of a long-running musical!

Rich Fruit Cake

¾ lb   Dark Brown Sugar
¾ lb   Butter
6   Eggs
1 lb   Flour
1 lb   Sultanas
1 lb   Currants
½ lb   Raisins
½ lb   Glacé Cherries
3 oz   Flaked Almonds (Crushed)
Pinch of Salt
½ Teason Mixed Spice
2 Tablespns Black Treacle
1 Sherry Glass of Brandy

Alan with HRH The Princess Royal

METHOD

Sieve together the flour salt & spice
Blend the sugar & butter together
Gradually mix in the fruit eggs brandy and almonds
Incorporate the dry ingredients and fruit to maintain
an even consistency
Add the black treacle towards the end of the mix
and finaly mix in the cherries the remaining eggs
and flour.
Bake in a 9/10 inch cake tin at Regulo 1 for approx
five to five and a half hours

This is the basic recipe used for the 75th Mikado,
Centenary Mikado, Centenary Pirates and the two
Doyly Carte reunion cakes.

Yours most sincerly

Alan

Mary as "Yum-Yum" with Alan and the cake he created for the 75th anniversary of *The Mikado* in 1960

Albert James

Albert was born in 1852 and his extraordinary career began in Mr D'Oyly Carte's "B" Company as a chorister in a double bill of *In The Sulks* and *The Pirates of Penzance*. In the "No.1 Patience" Company he played Major Murgatroyd and later took on the dual role of Stage Manager and Reginald Bunthorne for the "No.2 Company"! Also, in the "E" Company, he was Bunthorne again as well as the Lord Chancellor in *Iolanthe*, and both Stage Manager and Ko-Ko for the first tour of *The Mikado* during which one local critic described his performance as "better than George Grossmith in London".

He later rejoined the D'Oyly Carte's "B" troupe for *Haddon Hall*, *H.M.S. Pinafore* (Sir Joseph), *Utopia Ltd* and *The Chieftain*. Further duties included *The Rose of Persia*, *Trial by Jury* and the six month tour of South Africa. In later life, he became Director and Stage manager at the Savoy Theatre and subsequently Advance Publicity Manager for Helen D'Oyly Carte. He died (of exhaustion perhaps) in December 1913.

The recipe opposite was found in Albert's archive and is now part of the Melvyn Tarran Collection.
Above: a letter to Albert from W.S. Gilbert.

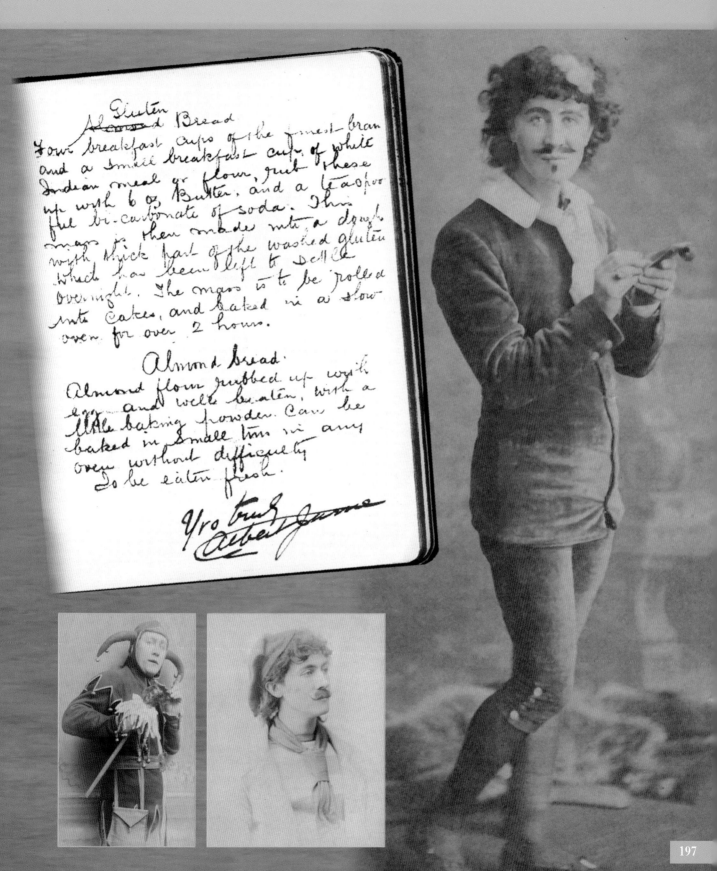

Gluten ~~Almond~~ Bread

Four breakfast cups of the finest bran and a small breakfast cup of white Indian meal or flour, rub these up with 6 oz Butter, and a teaspoonful bi-carbonate of soda. This mass is then made into a dough with thick part of the washed gluten which has been left to settle overnight. The mass is to be rolled into cakes, and baked in a slow oven for over 2 hours.

Almond Bread.
Almond flour rubbed up with eggs and well beaten, with a little baking powder. Can be baked in small tins in any oven without difficulty. To be eaten fresh.

Yrs truly
Albert James

George Grossmith

The legendary George Grossmith was the creator of many Gilbert and Sullivan "patter" roles – John Wellington Wells, Reginald Bunthorne, Lord Chancellor, King Gama, Ko-Ko, Robin Oakapple and Jack Point; he was also the Major General in the first London production of *The Pirates of Penzance*.

As a successful writer and composer his work included the popular *See me dance the Polka* performed, with many other original works, on mammoth tours of his one-man show which was also given by Royal Command at Balmoral Castle.

In 1892, he and his brother Weedon collaborated on the publication of *The Diary of a Nobody* – now regarded as a Victorian classic. Beyond G&S, he enjoyed only modest success in the West End but by many is regarded as the greatest of all Savoyards.

You should see me dance the Polka!

Geo: Grossmith

Children's Victorian Blancmange

In Grossmith's book The Diary of a Nobody, *Blancmange is served by Carrie Pooter, seemingly as part of a staple diet; the dish is sometimes ungratefully received by her family ...*

Ingredients

1 quart of milk; the yolks of four eggs; 3oz of ground rice; 6oz of pounded sugar;1 ½oz of fresh butter; the rind of one lemon; the juice of; 2 ½ oz of gelatine

Method

Make a custard with the yolks and ½ pint of the milk; pour into a basin. Put ½ the remaining milk into a saucepan with the ground rice, fresh butter, rind and 3oz of the sugar. Boil these ingredients until stiffened. Stir constantly. Add to the custard and mix them together well. Put the gelatine and remaining milk into a saucepan and stand by the side of the fire to melt; boil for a minute or two, stir into the basin and add 3oz more of pounded sugar. When cold, stir in the lemon juice (strained) and pour the mixture into a well-oiled mould. Avoid using the lemon peel. Set the mould in a pan of cold water until wanted for table.

Sandwiches

Princess Ida, Sandwiches

1/. worth from the local (pub)
evenly spread round the plate.
Some watercress for decoration.
Don't forget to hand them round.
Keep singing *and* chewing.
then drink a little and be
ready for the down beat.
If difficult ask for a rehearsal.

T. Penry Hughes.

A member of the D'Oyly Carte Opera Company for 19 years from 1922, playing small parts including the Notary, Foreman of the Jury, Bob Beckett and Annibale. At various times he covered for Darrell Fancourt, Richard Walker and Radley Flynn until leaving in 1941 to work for the war effort.

Anchovy and egg Sandwiches

12 anchovies
1 teaspoon curry powder
1 tablespoon butter, Cayenne to taste
  mustard and cress
    3 hard boiled eggs
    2 Tablespoons grated Parmesan cheese

Wash, bone & pound anchovies with egg yolks till smooth. Stir in curry powder, cheese, creamed butter & cayenne to taste. Spread filling with minced egg white & mustard & cress. Spread between slices of buttered brown bread or between split toast thinly buttered. Cut into fancy shapes. —

Dorothy Kingston.

Dorothy was born in 1912 and joined the D'Oyly Carte in 1932 as a chorister. She also played Kate in *The Yeomen of the Guard* and Lady Ella in *Patience*. Her understudy duties included a line in *The Sorcerer*. She left the Company in 1934 and went into the Sadler's Wells Opera from 1936–40.

Elsie Winnall & Ena Martin

Walnut Fudge

Almond Biscuits

Walnut Fudge

1 lb. brown sugar
½ lb. butter
1 tin Nestles milk
vanilla essence.
½ lb. walnuts.

Melt butter, add milk, sugar, nuts &
flavouring. Bring to boil. Then
boil briskly for twenty minutes
stirring all the while.

Elsie Winnall

Elsie spent five years in the D'Oyly Carte Chorus from 1932–37 and in her final season was given the small role of Ada in *Princess Ida*.

PICTON HALL (William Brown Street)
LIVERPOOL

Tuesday, September 27th, 1927, at 11 a.m.

PROMENADE CONCERT
BY
THE LIVERPOOL WIRELESS
ORCHESTRA

CONDUCTOR   Mr. FRED BROWN
VOCALIST   Miss ELSIE WINNALL

Programme

INTRODUCTION to 3rd Act "Lohengrin"   Wagner

OVERTURE—"Oberon"   Weber

"DEH VIENI, NON TARDAR" from "The Marriage of Figaro"   Mozart
Miss ELSIE WINNALL

SUITE "Peer Gynt"   Grieg
(a) Morning   (b) Death of Ase
(c) Anitra's Dance   (d) In the Hall of the Mountain King

TONE POEM—"Valse Triste"   Sibelius

VALSE SONG from "Romeo and Juliet"   Gounod
Miss ELSIE WINNALL

FANTASIA—"A Musical Jigsaw"   Ashton

Ena was a member of the D'Oyly Carte from 1929–34 and 1935–38. From 1932–39 she was married to Company bass baritone Richard Walker.

Almond Biscuits.
—

¼ lb butter
¼ " Castor Sugar.
6 oz Self-raising flour.
¼ lb ground almonds.
2 Eggs.

Cream together butter & sugar.
Stir in two well-whisked eggs,
gradually adding self-raising flour,
ground almonds & pinch of salt.
Mix well together until a stiff
paste is formed. Roll out about ¼ inch
cut into shapes, put on flat greased
tins, brush over with beaten egg
& milk & sprinkle with chopped
blanched almonds. Bake in a
moderate oven for 15 minutes, until
golden brown.

Ena Martin.

Norris's Lemonade

Especially for the children, our future Savoyards . . .

Lemonade: Feb: 25th 1935.

2 lemons   1 lb loaf sugar.
1 oz Citric Acid   1 Quart boiling water.

Peel lemons thinly & put peel into jug with sugar & boiling water. When cold add juice of lemons & citric acid. Oranges may be used instead of lemons in which case less sugar is required.

P. R. Norris

"With a halo of joy may their lives be surrounded" W.S. Gilbert. *The Sorcerer*

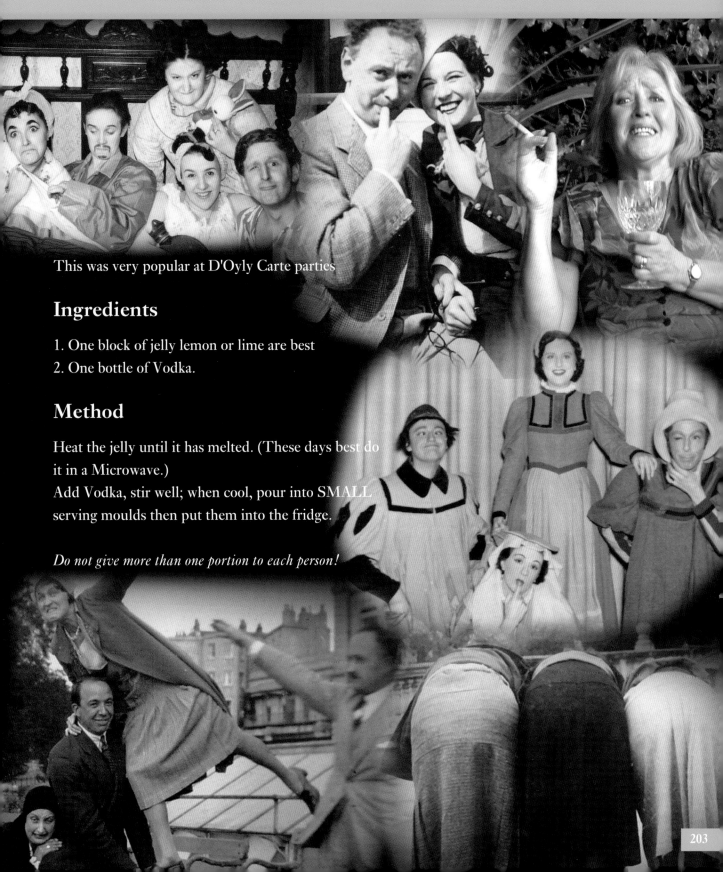

Very Naughty D'Oyly Carte Jelly

This was very popular at D'Oyly Carte parties

Ingredients

1. One block of jelly lemon or lime are best
2. One bottle of Vodka.

Method

Heat the jelly until it has melted. (These days best do it in a Microwave.)
Add Vodka, stir well; when cool, pour into SMALL serving moulds then put them into the fridge.

Do not give more than one portion to each person!

Martyn Green

S U N D R Y *Bunch*

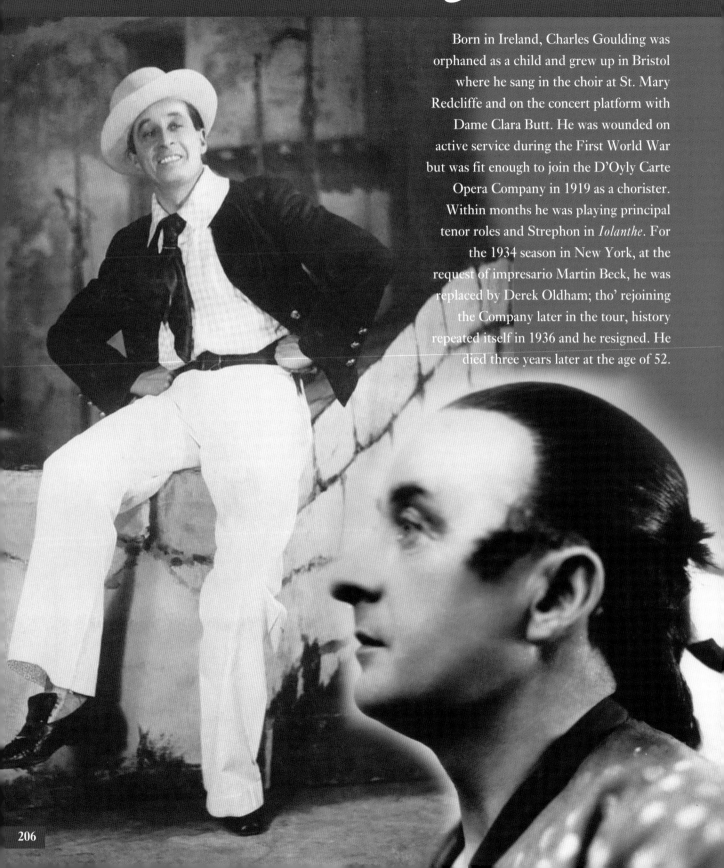

Charles Goulding

Born in Ireland, Charles Goulding was orphaned as a child and grew up in Bristol where he sang in the choir at St. Mary Redcliffe and on the concert platform with Dame Clara Butt. He was wounded on active service during the First World War but was fit enough to join the D'Oyly Carte Opera Company in 1919 as a chorister. Within months he was playing principal tenor roles and Strephon in *Iolanthe*. For the 1934 season in New York, at the request of impresario Martin Beck, he was replaced by Derek Oldham; tho' rejoining the Company later in the tour, history repeated itself in 1936 and he resigned. He died three years later at the age of 52.

Leichner Omelette

Gillian Knight.

Thomas Round

Donald Adams

Kenneth Sandford

Dorothy Gill.

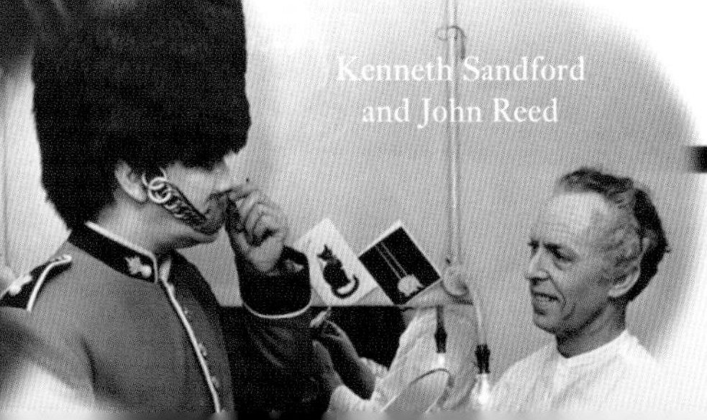

Kenneth Sandford and John Reed

Leichner omelette

2 Sticks No 5 greasepaint
1 "   " 9
½ " Carmine.

Squash between fingers. add
1 gill spirit gum & 1 glass
of whisky (if any) — call the
dresser — fireman — porter — police
& stage manager & sack 'em all.

Charles (Goulding)

Evelyn Gardiner demonstrates, to great effect, the subtle use of Leichner !!

Patricia Leonard & Michael Buchan

One of the Company's most versatile and popular artistes, Patricia joined in 1972, soon understudying and playing the entire mezzo repertory including Mrs Partlett in *The Sorcerer*, Elsa in *The Grand Duke* and her regular roles of Hebe, Lady Saphire, Leila and Peep-Bo. In 1977, convinced she was to be removed, she was unexpectedly asked to replace Lyndsie Holland as Principal Contralto and made her debut as the Fairy Queen in the new Silver Jubilee production of *Iolanthe*. From her initial performances, she found a new sympathy in these heavier roles – especially as Little Buttercup and Ruth – whilst her comedic skills made her an indescribably funny cello-playing Lady Jane and inebriated Baroness von Krankenfeldt. She remained with the D'Oyly Carte until 1982 and embarked on a hugely successful and busy freelance career until only a few months before her death in 2010.

After a striking debut with the Carl Rosa Opera Company at the age of nine, Michael was persuaded to turn fully professional in 1972 when he drove his wife, Patricia, to London for her audition at the Savoy and was himself invited to sing. He was a member of the Company for ten years, understudying John Ayldon and playing Bosun, Giorgio, Old Adam, Calynx and Samuel.

? ? ?

Pat's son Andrew as Ko-Ko's assistant, with John Reed

"Come bumpers, aye ever so many"

A Message from Michael ...

"David, dear boy, I am in shock! My dear Tricia and recipe books? I am amazed to see them mentioned together in the same sentence. No, no, no ... she was a wonderful person – a brilliant wit and crosswords solver, beautiful, a fantastic singer – but cook ???? Why, I well remember her first, and possibly the last banana jelly she attempted using a single square of gelatin and a pint of luke-warm water (with a large ripe banana, sliced and diced, dropped into it) placed on a shelf in the fridge for at least a week because it wouldn't set, and then heaved onto the garden compost heap. There are some things that stick in the memory, and others that you would rather did not – like a completely uncooked dinner with the Shoveltons! So I am sorry to say there are no recipes here, but would like to add that if the good Lord is fed up with her cooking I wish and pray he sends her back to me, for I miss her terribly."

Wilfred's Dog Biscuits & Ida's Bird Cake

(courtesy of Miss Peggy Ann Jones)

"In friendship's name"

Deidre Godfrey

"Dogs adore these, also cats if cut small enough – not the cats – the biscuits."

Peggy

Ingredients

8oz sausage meat
(or meat taken from sausages)
8oz plain wholemeal flour
2-3 fl.oz Stock or water

Method

Mix meat and flour well, bind with water to make a stiff dough, either roll out on floured surface to ½" thick and cut into shapes (I use a small pastry cutter in different shapes) or roll into sausage shapes about ½" long. Put onto a baking sheet and bake for about 30-50 mins (depending on size) until good and hard.

Sir Malcolm Sargent

♫ *"Oh willow, Tit-Willow, Tit-Willow"* ♫

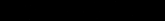

Bird Cake

2/3 scraps, bread, seeds, left overs etc,
1/3 melted fat or dripping.

Place in old yoghurt pot, and leave to set
in fridge, remove from pot, with scissors
or knife and the wild birds will love it.

Greatly respected as a choral conductor and best
remembered for his tenure as chief conductor at the
Proms, Sir Malcolm Sargent was associated with the
D'Oyly Carte Opera Company from 1926 to 1965. For
his debut at the Princes Theatre, he restored much
orchestral detail to performances from his studies of the
original autograph scores – to the extent that Rupert
D'Oyly Carte found it necessary to assure critics that the
modifications were indeed genuine and reflected the
composer's original orchestration. He returned to
conduct at the opening season of the rebuilt Savoy
Theatre, the Festival of Britain season, in 1961–62 (when
the copyright expired) and finally in 1963–64. He also
conducted thirteen of the Company's recordings and
remained a personal friend of Bridget D'Oyly Carte until
his death in 1967.

The Sir Malcolm Sargent Cancer Fund for Children
(now Clic Sargent) was established in his memory and in
aid of the charity, the D'Oyly Carte gave a performance
of *The Gondoliers* at Sadler's Wells in the presence of her
Majesty Queen Elizabeth the Queen Mother.

Alan E. Ward

Doctor Daly's Blessing

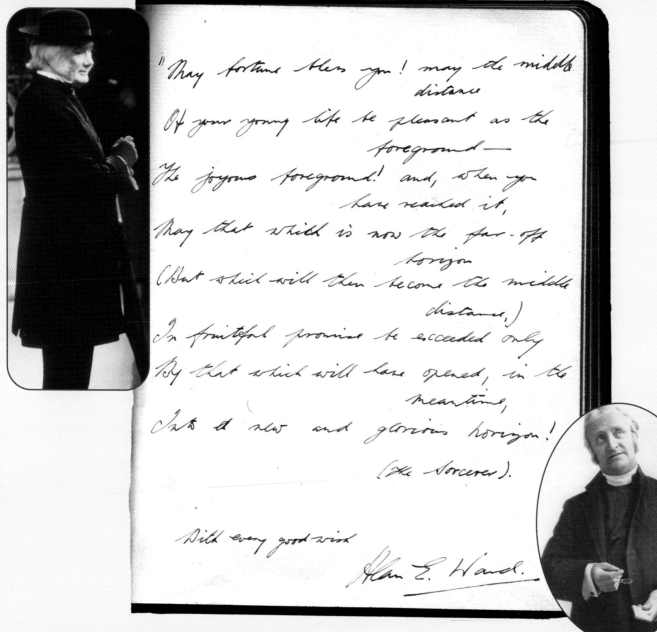

"May fortune bless you! may the middle distance
Of your young life be pleasant as the foreground —
The joyous foreground! and, when you have reached it,
May that which is now the far-off horizon
(But which will then become the middle distance,)
In fruitful promise be exceeded only
By that which will have opened, in the meantime,
Into a new and glorious horizon!

(The Sorcerer).

With every good wish

Alan E. Ward.

Alan E. Ward was Assistant Musical Director of the D'Oyly Carte Opera Company from 1930–41 and 1946–49. He also conducted a recording of G&S Overtures for RCA Victor, and *The Pirates of Penzance* with Martyn Green for RCA Victrola.

Happily I can play several instruments at once!" (Sorcerer d'da)
Sincerely

Alan E. Ward

Acknowledgements

The D'Oyly Carte Opera Trust For their generous consent to reproduce production photographs of the D'Oyly Carte Opera Company; special thanks to Ian Martin.

The National Portrait Gallery Portraits of Sir Henry Lytton, Bertha Lewis, Elsie Griffin and Sydney Granville.

The Lebrecht Photo Library Additional Photographs of Helen Gilliland (*The Gondoliers*), Winnie Melville and Derek Oldham (*The Yeomen of the Guard*).

The National Trust Messel family photograph.

John Reed and Nicholas Kerri Personal photographs of the D'Oyly Carte on tour 1955-79.

Mary Godfrey Archival material from the estate of Isidore Godfrey.

Cynthia Morey and Geoffrey Shovelton Additional Artwork and Caricatures.

Tony Joseph, Peter Parker, Chris Browne for their assistance in sourcing and supplying photographic material.

Fiona Canfield Photographs of Richard Suart at the English National Opera.

Ella Sampson Photo of Melvyn Tarran at Nymans

Paul Seeley Colour photographs of the 1981–82 D'Oyly Carte seasons.

Sheila Stanley The Flynn family recipes.

The Sir Arthur Sullivan Society Material for Sullivan pages.

Richard Swerrun Design Consultant and Editor.

Anthony Harris Social Media Website

Alexandra Sore Publicity & Press

David Stone "Who Was Who in the D'Oyly Carte Opera Company" – an invaluable reference website

Miles and Rachel at The Choir Press The "Lord (and Lady) High Everything Else".

and especially

Joyce Perry (Joy Garland) &

The Chefs of the D'Oyly Carte Opera Company.

Supporting Cast

Cover   Donald Adams

Page xvi   *Top*: The management! (*left to right*) Norman Meadmore*, William Cox-Ife (Chorus Master/Asst. To Isidore Godfrey), Robert Gibson (Director of Productions), David Palmer*, Bruce Worsley, Frederic Lloyd, Jerome Stephens (Stage Manager). (*Stage management team).

Middle: Peter Riley (Stage Manager) holds the cake celebrating the birthday of Tommy Appleby (next to Peter), Manager of the Opera House Manchester. Foreground: Gordon Mackenzie(Company Manager) (*left*) and John Reed (*right*).

Upper Right: Frederic Lloyd proposes a toast to John Reed on his 25th anniversary with the Company.

Lower Right: America 1955: Cynthia Morey, Muriel Harding, Jeffrey Skitch, Jennifer Toye and John Reed.

Bottom Left: Lunch Party at the home of Joyce Perry (Joy Garland) and Hugh Garland. (*incl*) Stanley Parker (*standing centre*), Leslie Rands (*right*); *seated*: Marjorie Eyre, Joy Garland and Muriel Dickson.

Bottom Right: Frederic Lloyd and Dame Bridget D'Oyly Carte.

Page 10   *Top Left*: taking tea with Sir Henry Lytton.

Page 14   Scenes from the life of Isidore Godfrey (*incl: lower centre*) his on-stage farewell at the Saville Theatre, 1968 and (*lower right*) conducting an open-air performance of "The Gondoliers" at Brockwell Park, London during the second world war.

Page 16   *Top*: On stage party at the Princes Theatre, London.

Page 17   Mad Margarets: (*left*) Patricia Leonard. (*right*) Joyce Wright, Marjorie Eyre, Peggy Ann Jones, (*colour shot*) Lorraine Dulcie Daniels.

Page 34   *Centre right photo*: On vacation with Jean Hindmarsh.

Page 36   *Bottom right*: Gillian with her husband Trevor Morrison (D'Oyly Carte Stage Carpenter).

Page 52   *Centre*: Beatrix Edwards (with Cynthia Morey and John Reed behind) (*right*) Beryl Dixon.

Page 55   *Top left*: "The Gondoliers" with Joyce Wright; (*centre left*) staged press photo with her family.

Page 60   *Bottom left*: "The Sorcerer" with Julia Goss.

Page 66   *Left*: Scenes from "Iolanthe", "La Vie Parisienne" and "The Count of Luxembourg".

Page 68   *Main picture* and *top right*: John Reed; (*bottom left*): Alan Styler as Cox in "Cox and Box"; cartoon by Cynthia Morey; (*bottom right*): Richard Watson as Pooh-Bah in "The Mikado".

Page 72   *Bottom right*: in concert with Geoffrey Shovelton

Page 84   Abby Hadfield; (*left*): Dick Whittington; (*top right*): D'Oyly Carte's Mikado with Peggy Ann Jones and Kenneth Sandford; collage; (*top*): Queen Rat; Apricot Crumble in Rapunzel (*right*); (*bottom*): Ethel in On Golden Pond; (*botton right*): Katisha.

Page 87   David Steadman (*left*) with Julia Goss, Gillian Knight, Kenneth Sandford, John Reed, Thomas Round and Donald Adams.

Page 102   *Bottom right*: meeting HRH The Duke of Edinburgh after a performance of "The Gondoliers"; with Lyndsie Holland, John Reed, Frederic Lloyd and Dame Bridget D'Oyly Carte.

Page 118   *Bottom left*: on tour with Eileen Bruckshaw, Isidore Godfrey and John Reed.

Page 120   As if the butter wouldn't melt . . . Joan Gillingham, Joyce Wright and Muriel Harding.

Page 124   *Top right*: Jane (*right*) with Roberta Morrell and Julia Goss; (*lower right*) with John Reed in "Iolanthe".

Page 128   *Top left*: Peggy is pictured left next to Joyce Perry (Garland); fellow chorister Gladys Bone stands on the right.

Page 130   *Bottom centre*: Donald recording the Mikado's song.

Page 138   *Centre top*: Inspired by the G&S opera Patience, this teapot was made by Royal Worcester in 1882. It is two sided – one with a man's face, the other with that of a woman and the base is inscribed as follows: "*Fearful consequences, through the laws of national selection and evolution of living up to one's teapot.*" Designed by R.W. Binns & James Hadley.

214

Top right: Sir Henry Lytton (*centre left*)- tea at the stage door canteen; (*right*) – Philip Potter, Jennifer Toye and Jean Hindmarsh.

Bottom left: a Boston tea party with Gillian Knight, Donald Adams, John Reed and Isidore Godfrey.

Bottom right: interval tea during a wartime performance of "The Gondoliers" at Brockwell Park; the Company includes Marjorie Eyre, Richard Walker, John Dean, Leslie Rands, Helen Roberts, Ella Halman, Isidore Godfrey and C.William Morgan.

Index of Featured Artists

"Finished! At Last! Finished!"

Reginald Bunthorne: *Patience*

David Steadman

"My mum, Cassie (a Londoner) and dad, Donald (a Brummie) met on Victoria Station when he was on leave from service in the Royal Engineers. They married in 1952 and I was born a respectable nine months later in a hospital in Wolverhampton, chosen because it could best deal with my mum's disability – a consequence of contracting polio as a child. It was some time before my father and I first met – he was serving in North Africa in my early months, and his eventual return meant a temporary move to army barracks in Darlington. As it happens, this was a somewhat safer environment for me, having been "forgotten" in my pram one hot sunny day and recovered in the nick of time from the garden of my grandparents' pub, suffering from severe sun-stroke! (I suffered again from this miserable state when attending a reception at the home of Benjamin Britten. We didn't speak much about music, but he had a couple of very good remedies for sunburn!).

I played the piano from the age of three; I would hear tunes on the radio and work out how to make the piano produce them. My parents believed they had a genius on their hands and sent me to have lessons with Mrs Edith Guttery L.R.A.M. of Amblecote, Stourbridge. She terrified me and to my horror, even agreed to continue teaching me in my lunch-breaks when I changed schools. Another plot foiled!

I blagged my way through my Royal Schools of Music exams and diplomas only to forget about music until I was asked to sing in the chorus of the Brierley Hill Grammar School production of *Iolanthe*. A school trip was arranged to see the D'Oyly Carte Opera Company perform the opera in Birmingham on 14 September 1966. Isidore Godfrey was conducting and I watched with fascination and an inexplicable degree of understanding. (Within weeks, I was conducting G&S records at home, using a knitting needle as a baton). Of course, without me realizing it, there they all were ... future friends and colleagues, extended family in some cases. As a music student in Birmingham, Bert Newby, the D'Oyly Carte Company Manager, often gave me a free ticket to watch the operas (by way of encouragement), but when asked about giving advice to a young musician who hoped one day to conduct the Company, Kenneth Sandford's response was 'DON'T!' I ignored his advice then, but later on cherished his friendship and support. Now that I am older, I have known the sadness of too many of them leaving us, but to all of them I owe grateful thanks for igniting the spark that has given me a modest, but joyous career. From that day in 1966, all I wanted to do was conduct in the theatre. Job done.

What I can't explain is how I came to be involved in producing a cook book. I have no interest in or appreciation of good food, have but a small repertoire of dishes I can cook and I eat only to stay alive. Perhaps, because Melvyn asked me, it was 'in friendship's name'."

Melvyn Tarran

"I was born in Bedford on 20 April 1938. After the war, my family moved to Kent and it was there that my appetite grew for a stage career. This was not to be however, and I went on to study Hotel and Catering Management.

After college, I continued my studies at the Ritz and Piccadilly Hotels in London; it was at the latter that I met a member of staff who had once played trombone in the D'Oyly Carte Orchestra and I was fascinated by his stories of the D'Oyly Carte Opera Company. This was how I came to see *Ruddigore*, my first Gilbert and Sullivan Opera, at Golders Green Hippodrome.

My career progressed: I served my National Service in the Army Catering Corps and went on to hold many senior management positions in the catering industry. My last was as Nationwide Head of Catering for a very large company, overseeing the expansion, refurbishment and daily operation of it's restaurants, coffee shops and both staff and outside catering. After nine years, I decided to build up my own company of licensed restaurants, tearooms and catering; my purchase of a large building adjacent to the National Trust Gardens at Sheffield Park in Sussex gave me the opportunity to cater for their thousands of visitors, numerous functions and also to present my popular G&S Sunday afternoon concerts as well as open a Gilbert and Sullivan Museum. This became the largest permanent collection on display in the world and was featured on television, radio and in magazines.

On retirement, I did not wish to give up my interest in G&S, so I invited a group of friends to form The Sussex Gilbert & Sullivan Society of which I became Chairman. Additionally, I am proud to have been invited to become a Vice-President of the London Gilbert & Sullivan Society.

I have been married to Kay for over fifty years and we now have four children and six grandchildren.

My friend David Steadman has been a tower of strength in getting this book published and contributing to it in his own special way. Without him, I would still be struggling on!"

Sunday concert at Oak Hall: Rebecca Knight and her mother Gillian with David and Melvyn. Rebecca had great success as one of the Opera Babes

Lord Hailsham and John Reed O.B.E.
Lord Hailsham served as Lord Chancellor from 1970–74 and 1979–1987;
John Reed was in office from 1959–1979 and at certain performances in 1981–82!